The Hermit in German Literature

UNC | COLLEGE OF ARTS AND SCIENCES
Germanic and Slavic Languages and Literatures

From 1949 to 2004, UNC Press and the UNC Department of Germanic & Slavic Languages and Literatures published the UNC Studies in the Germanic Languages and Literatures series. Monographs, anthologies, and critical editions in the series covered an array of topics including medieval and modern literature, theater, linguistics, philology, onomastics, and the history of ideas. Through the generous support of the National Endowment for the Humanities and the Andrew W. Mellon Foundation, books in the series have been reissued in new paperback and open access digital editions. For a complete list of books visit www.uncpress.org.

The Hermit in German Literature
From Lessing to Eichendorff

HENRY JOHN FITZELL

UNC Studies in the Germanic Languages and Literatures
Number 30

Copyright © 1961

This work is licensed under a Creative Commons CC BY-NC-ND license. To view a copy of the license, visit http://creativecommons.org/licenses.

Suggested citation: Fitzell, Henry John. *The Hermit in German Literature: From Lessing to Eichendorff.* Chapel Hill: University of North Carolina Press, 1961. DOI: https://doi.org/10.5149/9781469657493_Fitzell

Library of Congress Cataloging-in-Publication Data
Names: Fitzell, Henry John.
Title: The hermit in German literature : From Lessing to Eichendorff / by Henry John Fitzell.
Other titles: University of North Carolina Studies in the Germanic Languages and Literatures ; no. 30.
Description: Chapel Hill : University of North Carolina Press, [1961] Series: University of North Carolina Studies in the Germanic Languages and Literatures. | Includes bibliographical references.
Identifiers: LCCN 61064190 | ISBN 978-0-8078-8830-8 (pbk: alk. paper) | ISBN 978-1-4696-5749-3 (ebook)
Subjects: Hermits in literature. | Germanic literature — History and criticism.
Classification: LCC PD25 .N6 NO. 30 | DCC 830/ .93

PREFACE

To Dr. Walter Silz, Gebhart Professor of German Literature at Columbia University, I owe a frank and deep debt of gratitude. At Princeton in the recent past, his guidance, encouragement, indeed, his suggestion of the theme were responsible for my composing the study upon which this monograph is based.

In citing literary works or other studies, as well as in referring to them indirectly, I have indentified titles and authors clearly in my text, while the page or line number, act and scene, or chapter number, whichever was applicable, is bracketed next to the quotation or reference which it locates. For the specific editions cited, the reader is referred to the concise bibliography, arranged alphabetically by author and subdivided into (I) original texts and (II) critical and reference works. Accordingly, a large collection of notes is avoided in the hope that the body of the study may be rendered more lucid.

Finally I should like to thank the *German Quarterly* for its generous permission to include here material on Wieland's *Oberon* from an article of mine originally published in its pages. I am grateful to Dr. Kenneth Negus for his help in correcting proof, and I express my sincere thanks to the Research Council of Rutgers University for its generous grant in support of this study.

JOHN FITZELL

TABLE OF CONTENTS

INTRODUCTION XI

CHAPTER I   THE HERMIT OF LITERARY TRADITION 1

Wolfram and Grimmelshausen.

CHAPTER II   THE HERMIT AND SOCIETY 10

(1) Lessing: Der Eremit, p. 10 (2) Goethe: Satyros, p. 13 (3) Lenz: Die Kleinen, p. 19 (4) Klinger: Sturm und Drang, p. 26 (5) Bürger: Der wilde Jäger, p. 31 (6) Lessing: Nathan der Weise, p. 36 (7) Chamisso: Peter Schlemihl, p. 47.

CHAPTER III   THE INNER CONFLICT 54

A. (1) Goethe: Erwin und Elmire, p. 54 (2) Lenz: Der Waldbruder, p. 59 (3) Klinger: Die Zwillinge, p. 64 (4) Brentano: Godwi, p. 66 (5) Droste-Hülshoff: Walter, p. 71 (6) Lenau: Die Marionetten, p. 77.
B. (1) Klinger: Fausts Leben, Thaten und Höllenfahrt, p. 80 (2) Wackenroder: Ein wunderbares morgenländisches Märchen, p. 82 (3) Hoffmann: Serapion, p. 83.

CHAPTER IV   THE HERMIT AND NATURE 88

(1) Wieland: Oberon, p. 88 (2) Hölderlin: Hyperion, p. 95 (3) Novalis: Heinrich von Ofterdingen, p. 101 (4) Schiller: Die Braut von Messina, p. 105 (5) Uhland: König Eginhard, p. 106 (6) Kerner: Die Heimatlosen, p. 108 (7) Goethe: Faust, p. 111 (8) Eichendorff: Eine Meerfahrt, p. 114.

CHRONOLOGICAL TABLE OF WORKS 120

BIBLIOGRAPHY 121

INDEX 124

INTRODUCTION

A very strong penchant toward inwardness or "Innerlichkeit", a tendency to withdraw from the outer, social world to the "world within" is generally characteristic of German literature. Novalis spoke for more than German Romanticism when he said, "Nach innen geht der geheimnisvolle Weg. In uns oder nirgends ist die Ewigkeit mit ihren Welten, die Vergangenheit und Zukunft." In all literary genres of German literature in all periods we note a concentration upon the inner reactions of the individual to the forces at work outside him.

Indeed, the world is recreated from within and we see life revealed and interpreted through a creative process in the individual personality. This is, to be sure, the very cardinal principle of artistic expression. Nature and society appear as the very expressions of the inner self in its longing for harmony with a higher order. Several remarks by Fritz Strich in his essay, *Natur und Geist der deutschen Dichtung* (*Die Ernte*: *Franz Muncker zu seinem 70. Geburtstage* – see Bibliography), illustrate this idea very pointedly. Strich contrasts, for example, the nordic landscape with that of classical Greece (p. 8), and says that the nordic landscape was not "menschlich beseelt", that one could not imagine in it the presence of such gods as those inhabiting the sunny hills and groves of Greece. He later describes the Germanic gods as "nebelhaft", as "Wanderer", and declares (p. 8), "Der Mensch konnte nicht nach aussen, sondern musste nach innen gewendet sein." A subsequent passage in the same essay contrasts Parzifal with Dante (p. 9). While Dante is led by Virgil, the spirit of classicism, Parzifal searches out his way to God along lonely, untrodden paths, guided only by the faith ("Triuwe" or "Hingabe") in his heart and the never-slacking power of his will. Professor Strich sees the position of the German poet thus (p. 20): "Seine Frage an die Welt ist die: wie wird sie von seinem Helden erlebt, und so kommt es hier denn nur auf den inneren Reichtum des Menschen an." This contrast of classic and romantic types (subsequently developed and expanded into a full volume)[1] derives actually from Ludwig Uhland's essay, *Über die Romantik*. Indeed, Professor Strich literally paraphrases Uhland most fre-

[1] *Deutsche Klassik und Romantik*, Bern 1949.

quently – without referring to him. Uhland's (and Professor Strich's) conviction is not tenable – namely the conviction that the dweller in Germanic landscapes had to turn inward because he had not the clear outlines, the clear conceptions of gods as illumined in the sunny climes of Greece. This theory stems largely, in fact, from the lack of plastic art portraying the gods, for example, in the North – a lack due in turn, rather to a scarcity of substantially permanent materials such as the marbles of the south. Those relics of ancient Germanic art which remain are mostly small objects of metal, otherwise wooden fragments, some carvings and inscriptions on stone (cf. *e. g.* the illustrations in Jan de Vries' two volume *Altgermanische Religionsgeschichte*).

Yet the figure of the hermit does embody the undeniably characteristic inwardness attributed by Professor Strich to German literature and art (Dürer's St. Jerome), and it is therefore not surprising that the recluse early became a favorite figure in literature. What is surprising is that his character and role have not hitherto been made the subject of more concentrated interpretation and investigation. This gap the present study seeks to fill.

The hermit must be defined as one who withdraws from society to achieve a deeper understanding of life through solitary contemplation. The causes and circumstances of his withdrawal reveal to varying extents his "Weltanschauung". *Der grosse Brockhaus* defines hermits ("Anachoreten" or "Zurückgezogene", "Eremiten" or "Einsiedler") as "in der Einsamkeit lebende Mönche im Christentum seit Ausgang des dritten Jahrhunderts –." The lives of these ascetics were characterized traditionally by "Ringen mit Sexualverdrängung, Phantasiegebilden, Dämonenkampf". Under "Weltflucht" we find in the *Schweizer Lexikon* the following definition: "eine einsame Lebensweise frommer Menschen, die sich zu innerer Sammlung und religiöser Übung einzeln (Einsiedler) oder gruppenweise (Mönchtum) in die (nie absolute) Abgeschiedenheit von der Welt zurückgezogen haben, oft beeinflusst von einer pessimistischen Beurteilung des Lebens in der Welt." These definitions we shall see illustrated variously in our own subsequent investigations.

In his work, *The Hermit in English Literature from the Beginnings to 1660*, (p. 18 ff. – see Bibliog.), Charles P. Weaver notes some general distinctions between the anchorite and the hermit. The anchorite was required to pass through a trial period of fasting and prayer before being ceremoniously installed in his cell. The abode of the anchorite was generally connected with a church or cloister. His life was more strictly regulated than that of the hermit; the anchorite could be attended by those who were committed to bringing him the bare necessities of life, but he was dedicated to remaining in his cell, secluded from the world, until death released him.

The hermit removed himself to the forest or mountains to a life of solitary contemplation, but, unlike the anchorite, he was not severely confined to his dwelling. He occupied himself very often with studies of various sorts – for example, the healing powers of herbs – and he could cultivate the land about his abode, even keep animals. The hermit also provided hospitality to wanderers in need of shelter, and he was not forced to forswear all contact with the outside world. Unlike the anchorite, he was not, as a rule, of clerical status. The distinctions between hermit and anchorite made by Weaver are valid also for German literature and his descriptions of their modes of life are generally applicable, as we shall see, not only to English, but to all solitaries in the Christian tradition. The first two hermit figures to be discussed provide examples more than adequate to support this conviction.

The criteria which we have used in selecting figures from a period extending, roughly, from Lessing to the death of Goethe are twofold. First of all, the hermit figure, even if not plainly designated as such, must voluntarily withdraw from society, although not necessarily permanently, at the same time revealing his motivation to do so, and he must express a "Weltanschauung" (hence play an important role in the work in which he occurs). Second, I have tried to include only works which undeniably possess literary value and interest. Perhaps we must apologize for a certain arbitrariness in our choice of figures. The study does not claim completeness, yet it is nearly so. Only two major works have been excluded – Tieck's *Sternbald* and Eichendorff's *Ahnung und Gegenwart*. The solitaries in these novels are represented better as types and presented more interestingly as characters by the Brentano and Eichendorff works in our study.

It has seemed most practical for concentrated analysis and interpretation to arrange the works in comprehensive thematic-groups, under rubrics which describe generally the themes associated with the figures analysed. The works under each separate rubric are chronologically arranged.

CHAPTER I

THE HERMIT OF LITERARY TRADITION

Wolfram's *Parzifal* and Grimmelshausen's *Simplicissimus* contain the most important portrayals of the hermit in German literature prior to the eighteenth century. These two works are in themselves the most important single literary expressions of their respective ages, the age of chivalry and the baroque era. The role of the hermit in each of these works displays the characteristics of Goethe's "Urpflanze" with all its potentialities of development. Indeed, many of the qualities and themes associated with the hermits of these works are revealed in similar figures by poets of subsequent periods (particularly in Romanticism) varying, of course, with the individual creative personality and the movement or age in which he writes.

Essential to an interpretation of the hermit's role in Wolfram's poem is an understanding of his deepened concepts of "Minne" and "Triuwe". For Wolfram these ideals represent psychological and ethical values of a profoundly religious nature. Near the beginning of the pivotal ninth book (Str. 435, 1. 79 ff.), Parzifal reencounters his cousin, Sigune[1], who appears fittingly here as a female recluse (Klausnerin) mourning her dead betrothed, Schionatulander. This episode reveals with the utmost clarity and simplicity the profound sense which the poet instills into "Minne" and "Triuwe". Sigune retains scarcely a vestige of her former beauty, for she has withered in her grief and in atonement for the caprice which sent Schionatulander to his death in combat. This capricious vanity and its tragic result render Sigune guilty of corrupting the ideal of "Minne" as understood in its usual courtly connotation. Now, in solitude, her repentance and atonement are connected with Wolfram's concept of a new and true "Minne" – (440, 1. 211 ff.)

"mîner jaemerlîchen zîte jâr
wil ich im minne geben für wâr;
der rehten minne ich pin sîn wer –."

The woman who remains loyal to her husband for the duration of

---

[1]. Wolfram's choice of name has significance. In Germanic mythology, Sigune was the wife of the fire god, Loki. When chained to a rock beneath the dripping venom of a serpent, he was comforted by Sigune, who remained loyally at his side to catch the poison in a cup.

his life fulfills the generally accepted ideal of "Minne" (436, 1. 100 ff.); yet after his death she would normally be free to bestow her grace elsewhere. Sigune remains bound to Schionatulander in an eternal "Minne" which embodies the deep sense of "Triuwe", conveying repentance and atonement.

This preliminary episode of the ninth book acts as an introduction to Parzifal's stay with Trevrizent in that it clarifies the aspect of atonement implicit in the full realization necessary for complete repentance. Sigune, the recluse, expiates her guilt under the sign of "Minne" which also becomes "Hingabe" (Triuwe). This is symbolized in the ring, Schionatulander's pledge, which she still wears – (440, 1. 225) – "daz ist ob mîner triuwe ein sloz."

Before considering the figure of Trevrizent and his role in the poem, we must recall briefly the salient features of the "Gralgemeinschaft". Although the society of the Grail is knightly in character, it is so in the same sense in which Wolfram has deepened the ideal of "Minne". It represents a synthesis of the knightly and the purely religious elements. The guardians of the Grail are knights, and courtly ladies follow the Grail in procession. The sacred object, itself, may be borne only by the purest maiden (Parzifal's aunt, Repans de Schoie). There are no conventionally sacred symbols in the society, for even the Grail, itself, is, at least outwardly, a kind of stone. The traditional cross is nowhere apparent, although the dove, which replenishes the powers of the Grail to maintain the eternal youth of its guardians, assumes an equivalent importance. Only the king is permitted to wed, while the knights must forswear worldly "Minnedienst". Thus, religious and knightly ideals are welded into a unique and deeply symbolic hierarchy over which Parzifal is destined to reign (500, end).

When Trevrizent describes the folly of Anfortas and the consequences of it, the reason for his own withdrawal and the purpose in his life as a hermit are made plain. Anfortas, the youthful Grail king, had committed excesses in the pursuit of "Minnedienst" which were expressly forbidden by the Grail edict. The poisoned tip of a heathen lance had dealt him a wound which would not heal and which left him suspended in a living death of unending pain. This misfortune was felt to be a divine punishment, for all cures proved to be of no avail – (478, 1, 1363)

> "swelch grâles hêrre ob minne gert
> anders dann diu schrift in wert.
> der muoz es komen ze arbeit
> und in siufzebaeriu herzeleit."

Henceforth Anfortas has lived only in the hope of redemption through the question which is to release him from his agony. Trevrizent has betaken himself to the forest to atone for his brother's sin by rejecting knighthood and praying for him – (480, 1. 1420 ff.)

> "dâ lobet ich der gotes kraft,
> daz ich deheine rîterschaft
> getaete niemer mêre,
> daz got durch sîn êre
> mînem bruoder hulfe von der nôt."

Trevrizent stands between Anfortas and Parzifal. On the one hand, he atones for his brother's sin and prays for his redemption. On the other hand, he is in the unique position of being able to make his nephew conscious of the nature of his guilt – thus indirectly bringing about the release of Anfortas through Parzifal.

The nature of Parzifal's guilt is inextricably involved with the idea of his relationship to the Grail hierarchy, which Trevrizent definitively clarifies. Parzifal's mother was the sister of Anfortas and Trevrizent; Parzifal, himself, is the natural heir to the Grail, since he is the only direct male descendant of the immediate ruling family. The way to repentance is opened by Trevrizent when he refers to the killing of Ither, and Parzifal admits, in turn, to being the killer. His guilt consists of a kind of original sin, for it was not wittingly incurred. His sins were three. He had killed Ither, his kinsman by marriage, caused the untimely death of his mother by deserting her (499), and he had not been moved to inquire the reason for the suffering of Anfortas.

It must be emphasized that the major portion of Parzifal's guilt lies precisely in the fact that he has harmed his own flesh and blood and, through them, the Grail and God. Possessing the knowledge which Trevrizent imparts to him. Parzifal can repent. Trevrizent absolves his nephew – (500, end)

> "er sprach: gip mir dîn sünde her:
> vor gote ich bin dîn wandels wer –"

and, by once more opening Parzifal's way to the Grail, he indirectly accomplishes the salvation of Anfortas.

Just as the ideals "Minne" and "Triuwe" possess a deeper meaning which is both worldly and religious, so, too, the Grail with its company represents a blending of chivalrous form and religious spirit. Trevrizent, however, as a hermit, embodies this synthesis. Although he impresses upon Parzifal the fact that he is a layman (462, 1. 881), Trevrizent absolves his nephew of sin. In spite of the Grail edict which forbids its knightly guardians to practice "Frauenminne", Trevrizent lauds the chivalrous life, and he describes in great detail (495-500) and with pride his own earlier pursuit of "Aventiure" throughout the known world. From his lips resound the familiar lines, "swer schildes ambet ueben wil, der muoz durchstrichen lande vil". There is no tone of contempt or criticism in his words when he speaks of the society which he has given up, but rather praise of it and pride in his past experience (even though Trevrizent has been only less guilty than Anfortas in forgetting the edict of the Grail).

Yet he has rejected the practice of knighthood and withdrawn as a hermit to atone for his brother's guilt. This function of hermithood as a vicarious atonement for other men's sins is, of course, akin to the conceptions of Christ and of sainthood; it is a theme frequently encountered in connection with other figures also (cf. Lenz's *Die Kleinen* – Chap. II). The synthesis of the worldly and the religious elements in Trevrizent render him qualified to act as Parzifal's spiritual tutor and to lift from him frustration and guilt of the past.

While Trevrizent stands in the center of Wolfram's poem, the figure of the hermit is encountered at the outset and at the conclusion of Grimmelshausen's *Simplicissimus*. Even though we have the father as a hermit at the beginning of the novel, and the son at the end, it may be said that the conception of the hermit, as such, forms a frame around the violently colorful, but chaotic age which Grimmelshausen so vividly brings to life. This significant detail in the form of the novel expresses a great deal about the author's reaction to his times. Grimmelshausen lived in no such period as Wolfram's with its firmly established knightly culture. Instead he saw a world, in which human values were utterly disregarded, quaking at its ethical foundations.

The hermit (Simplicius' father, who is introduced in Book I, chapter six) renounces the world completely because of disgust and horror for it built up through the sad experiences of his past. To save his soul, he dedicates his remaining years to preparing for the life to come. His son, of whose identity he is unaware, cannot benefit fully by the religious instruction imparted to him because he has been reared in ignorance and in conditions only slightly above the animal. It is necessary for Simplicius to experience war and the degeneration of every sort that accompanies it until there is produced in him precisely the same horror and fear for his soul that drove his father into solitude.

Although the scriptural lessons and the last advice of the hermit to Simplicius have no immediate practical meaning for the inexperienced lad, he is (like Parzifal in his reaction to his mother's advice) impressed by them and they remain with him throughout his worldly life. Their full effect is realized when Simplicius, himself, rejects the world and its vanities.

We know from the pastor's account (I, ch. 22) how Simplicius' father, a high-ranking officer, arrived at the parsonage door in the dead of night, his rich dress spattered with blood, sword still in hand, after the battle at Höchst. Later the governor of Hanau informs the pastor (I, ch. 23) that he had believed his brother-in-law dead. He had sent out soldiers to find his sister, only to discover that she had been abducted by imperial cavalry and taken, in turn, from them by peasants in the Spessart.

The heartbroken officer was in despair because of the lost battle, because he had lost his wife after only one year of marriage together with the child she was about to bear, and because he, himself, had not perished defending the gospel. He turned over all his worldly possessions to the pastor, even including the golden chain with a miniature of his wife, which he exchanged for the pastor's wagon chain – a complete renunciation of the life he had known. With only a few household utensils and a miserable wool blanket to cover his nakedness, he left for the most obscure part of the forest. The pastor sums up the motives of the recluse, when he says to Simplicius (I, ch. 22), "Sein geistiger Sinn und widerwertige Begegnüssen hemmeten endlich den Lauff seiner weltlichen Glückseligkeit so, dass er seinen Adel und ansehenliche Güter in Schotten, da er gebürtig, verschmähet und hindann setzet, weil ihm alle Welthandel abgeschmack, eitel und verwerfflich vorkamen. Er verhoffte, mit einem Wort, seine gegenwärtige Hoheit umb eine künftige bessere Glory zu verwechseln, weil sein hoher Geist einen Eckel an allem zeitlichen Pracht hatte und sein Dichten und Trachten war nur nach einem solchen erbärmlichen Leben gerichtet, darinn du ihn im Wald angetroffen und biss in seinen Todt Gesellschaft geleistet hast." (The pastor also supposes that the hermit may have been influenced in this direction by the reading of "popish" books about the lives of ancient hermits.) The motivation for hermithood in this case is a "Verleidung der Welt" – as well as the "jenseitig" – Christian urge to prepare for a better life after death; this hermit figure is, to a large extent, explainable by the terrible conditions in Germany during the period of the Thirty Years War.

Simplicius learns much later through a chance meeting with his "Knan" (V, ch. 8) that his spiritual father was in fact his real sire, "Capitain" Sternfelss von Fuchsheim. After the battle at Nördlingen, Susanna Ramsay, the Hanau governor's sister, and mother of Simplicius, had escaped from the imperial troops in the neighborhood of Simplicius' boyhood home. The "Knan" was no sooner able to help her from her horse and procure the aid of his wife and hired girls, than the unfortunate lady perished in child-birth leaving a legacy of some jewelry for her son, whom she committed into the peasant's care.

It is necessary to bear in mind with regard to Simplicius' development and Grimmelshausen's "Weltanschauung" that the ignorance of the hero is almost a prerequisite for the eventual assimilation of the hermit's instruction. Simplicius readily grasps reading and writing, and he also grasps the importance of the lessons in religion. The message of the religious instruction can only become clear in proportion as the hero becomes worldly-wise. This is its limitation, by nature, and, at the same time, its value. Simplicius is profoundly impressed by the hermit's tutelage; of that there can be no doubt – so much so, that these lessons eventually decide the outcome of his life – (I, ch. 9) "denn dass ich alles so bald gefasst, was mir der fromme Einsidel vorgehalten, ist daher kommen, weil er die geschlichte Tafel meiner Seelen gantz laer und ohn einige zuvor hinein gedrückte Bildnüssen gefunden –".

The hermit realizes that his young charge is not likely to remain alone in the forest when he, himself, has died and before lying down in his grave he recapitulates the ideas which he wishes imprinted upon the open pages of the boy's soul (I, ch. 12). Instead of screaming and howling at their parting, Simplicius is to remember, even though he grow as old as Methusalah, that he must never cease trying to know himself for what he is – for the basic reason underlying the damnation of all is that men recognize neither what they have been, nor what they might have become. Simplicius must also avoid evil society and remain constant and true to himself under all circumstances; he who persists in these principles to the end of his life will become blessed and, like the phoenix of Grimmelshausen's frontispiece verses, be reborn through fire.

For Simplicius, the hermit exemplifies these moral lessons. He has learned to know himself and consequently he has virtually shunned not only the temptations of all human company, but he has also fled from the world, itself – (I, ch. 12)" – ist auch in solchem Vorsatz biss an das Ende verharret, an welchem ohn Zweiffel die Seeligkeit hangt –."

Throughout the myriad adventures in which he vacillates between good and evil, the hero is never actually in doubt as to what is right, for the seed planted by his hermit father had taken root in his conscience, and kept it alive. As a marauding mercenary, Simplicius is always horrified by the depravity of his evil genius, Olivier, while, in the company of Hertzbruder, he also acutely perceives his own shortcomings. In the opening chapter of the fifth and final book, Simplicius and Hertzbruder make a pilgrimage to Einsiedeln, and Hertzbruder insists that they walk with peas in their shoes as part of their penance. Simplicius cooks his peas in Schaffhausen and arrives comfortably in Zurich, where Hertzbruder discovers his friend's deceit. Simplicius had undertaken the journey only for the sake of accompanying Hertzbruder and with no thought of penance for his past sins. Hertzbruder warns him that his soul is in danger, and that their friendship cannot continue while Simplicius refuses to better himself in the eyes of God.

Immediately the past wells up before his eyes and he thinks of the copious evil pranks which he has executed. Following Hertzbruder in humility, he laments inwardly the innocence lost when he came out of his hermit's forest abode into a corrupt and depraved world.

In the Mummelsee episode (V, ch. 12-17) the chaos which mankind has created in the world is contrasted with the divine order of nature. The hero comes to the lake spirits who are, in a sense, personified natural forces. They are not transitory spirits, for their existence is as constant as that of earth. Yet, although they are free of all the ills which beset mankind, they possess no eternal soul, no potentiality of attaining heavenly bliss, as does man, who seems to concentrate upon deserving damnation. The king of the Mummelsee sylphs is deeply troubled over the question of future existence, since, if mankind in its depravity so angers God that He brings the world to an end, nature, itself, must logically perish. The king demands to know the truth about man's behaviour and Simplicius lies to him.

The various callings of society, the classes, the trades – all of them he describes as carrying out their offices in the most exemplary manner, but Simplicius concludes his account (V, ch. 15, end) with bitter sarcasm which transparently lets the truth shine through. There is no lassitude in serving God, but, rather, all men vie with one another in attempting to do so in the most righteous manner – for that very reason the world is disrupted by religious wars. Each party insists that the other is on the wrong path. There are no more misers to be met with, but only the thrifty, no spendthrifts, but, instead, the generous. One finds no cutthroats robbing and murdering, only soldiers who protect their native land. Beggars are now those who despise riches and love voluntary poverty.

The burden of the episode (and of the novel) is that the evils of society constitute a crime against nature and the divine order. After travels throughout the European continent, Asia, and upon the sea, concluding with pilgrimages to Rome and to Loreta in Spain, Simplicius turns to his books. All of these experiences serve only to ripen in him the resolution to save his soul as his father did by rejecting the world.

When he reads the advice of the apollonian oracle to the Roman legates, "Nosce te ipsum", his hermit-father's last words (I, ch. 12) echo out of the forest of his bygone innocence. Simplicius sees himself – (V. 23) "Solches (Erkenne dich selbst!) machte, dass ich mich hindersonne und von mir selbst Rechnung über mein geführtes Leben begehrte; weil ich ohne das müssig war, da sagte ich zu mir selber, dein Leben ist kein Leben gewesen, sondern ein Todt, deine

Tage ein schwerer Schatten, deine Jahr ein schwerer Traum, deine Wollust schwere Sünden, deine Jugend eine Phantasey und deine Wolfahrt ein Alchimisten Schatz, der zum Schornstein hinauss fährt –."

At the conclusion of the novel, Simplicius cites the words of Guevara, a Spanish novelist whom he has been reading; they impress him by their force and conviction, and express adequately a summation of his own experience – (V, ch. 24) "Alsdenn wird die arme Seel sagen: Verflucht seystu Welt! weil ich durch dein Anstifften Gottes und meiner selbst vergessen und dir in aller Üppigkeit, Bossheit, Sünd und Schand die Tag meines Lebens gefolgt hab –." Thus, like his father, Simplicius thrusts human society from him, and becomes a hermit to save his soul from otherwise certain damnation.

The principal point of contrast between the figures of Trevrizent and Simplicius is illuminated by their respective motives for rejecting society. Trevrizent becomes a hermit to atone for his brother's sin. In his action there is no criticism of the world as he has known it. To give up the knightly life, as such, is, for Trevrizent, a personal sacrifice which he willingly brings in service to a higher ideal (the Grail) embodying the purest elements of knighthood and the spirit of Christ. By their departure from a chaotic and corrupt world, Simplicius and his father proclaim the unconquerable vitality of the individual to look into himself and save the soul from damnation. Thus, we may say that Trevrizent's withdrawal represents a positive aspect of hermithood, while that of Simplicius and his father represents a negative one. The positive aspect in *Parzifal* has its roots in the idealistic world of knighthood and the negative aspect in Simplicissimus is a product of the sordid, savage world of the Thirty Years War – the hermit figure becomes very frequently a social "Gradmesser", a criterion of historical and social conditions.

Trevrizent is a hermit in the service of a high ideal, while, for Simplicius and his father, living is a struggle to attain personal salvation. For Trevrizent the knightly life, although praiseworthy for its own sake, is also dedicated to an ideal even more sublime. For Simplicius earthly life is a marsh of sin from which the soul must learn to extricate itself at all costs.

There are many characteristics which are common to both Trevrizent and Simplicius. Most obvious, but none the less significant, is the fact that both flee into solitude where the soul is closest to the pervading spirit. Both Trevrizent and Simplicius become hermits after having lived lives rich in experience (whether it be recalled with pride and nostalgia, or in horror and contempt).

The hermits of both Wolfram and Grimmelshausen (Simplicius' father) act as educators qualified by full knowledge of the world.

In both the epic of chivalry, *Parzifal*, and the baroque novel, *Simplicissimus*, the hermits are closely related to the characters upon whom they exercise decisive influence. The hermits in both of these works spend the remainder of their lives humbly close to nature, nourishing themselves with herbs and acorns and such vegetables as they are able to cultivate around their mean dwelling places. Above all, they each comprise a most concentrated presentation of the individual in conflict with the collective aspect of the world and, of course, too, with his own soul.

Many of the characteristic themes and motifs associated with the figures examined in this chapter are given deeper and more poetic, psychological, or metaphysical significance, especially in *Storm and Stress* and *Romanticism*, where, for example, the role of nature assumes such profound meaning.

CHAPTER II

THE HERMIT AND SOCIETY

This phase of our study deals with those works illustrating the relationship of the hermit to society and the causes for his withdrawal from it; it deals, also, with the poet's conception of the hermit in contrast to specific aspects of the world about him. Naturally, in certain works, such as *Satyros* or *Sturm und Drang*, the role and interpretation of nature supply the cause area of conflict between the hermit and society, while in *Sturm und Drang* it is the reaction to an aspect of society which leads Blasius to the discovery of a dynamic nature – and it must be emphasized that this characteristic discovery is surely the most significant contribution of the Storm and Stress to the interpretation of individual experience in the entire Goethe period. The importance of the hermit figure, in this part of the study, lies in his relationship to society, his reaction to it, and the consequent direction which he takes.

(1) Lessing's little tale in verse, *Der Eremit*, is by no means one of his more significant artistic creations, yet it does have a relative importance which is not at first apparent. Even at the age of twenty (1749) when the poem was written, Lessing was already inclined toward the humanistic-religious thinking which was to attain its full artistic fruition in *Nathan der Weise*. (Two other works of a serious religious nature were conceived during this same early period of activity as a critic in Berlin – *Die Religion*, a didactic poem with "Vorerinnerung" and the first of his theological essays, *Gedanken über die Herrnhüter*.)

The figure of the hermit, himself, shows none of the traits associated, for example, with Trevrizent or Simplicissimus. In fact, Lessing's hermit is as much the butt of his creator's wit as is the society with which he unfortunately comes into contact. We do not learn the reasons for his initial rejection of the world, nor can we characterize his attitude toward society as other than that of a charlatan. The poet's interest in the characters in the poem is that of a critical narrator and commentator who stands outside the course of development; we do not, in this instance, perceive the world as inwardly experienced by the hermit, but, rather, we see the effect of the hermit as a poseur upon a weak and susceptible society.

His mode of life (1. 25-40) follows the traditions we have already observed in the definitions in the introduction. He dwells in a tiny, bare hut in the thick of the forest, and, taking no meat or wine, he subsists on roots and water (like Trevrizent and Simplicissimus). The tone of the verses seems to reveal that the acts of religious devotion which the hermit performs are nothing more than sham – entirely devoid of any deeper meaning –

(1. 27 ff.) "Was je ein Eremit getan,
Fing er mit grösstem Eifer an.
Er betete, er sang, er schrie,
Des Tags, des Nachts, und spät und früh."

He scourges himself until he bleeds, fasts, and stands on one foot in his spurious efforts to attain heavenly bliss.

As might be expected, the zeal of the young hermit soon becomes known to the inhabitants of near-by Kerapolis (or "Hörnerstadt"). The first of the many pilgrims to the hermitage is a trembling, elderly woman on crutches. She spreads the reputation of the hermit among the women of the city, who come to consider the pilgrimage to the holy man a cardinal prerequisite of true piety –

(1. 77 ff.) "Der ist verloren und verflucht,
Der unsern Eremiten nicht besucht!"

Consequently, the young and pretty women of the city also follow their neighbor's example in the edification of the soul. To the old and ugly the hermit speaks of death, vanity, and reverence, and to the poor of heavenly joy, but, with his pretty visitors, he speaks of love, the basic Christian virtue. This concept, however, is quickly stripped of its spiritual value, and brought down to a fleshly niveau. When the young women visit him, the hermit shows his true nature –

(1. 163 ff.) "Ich hätte manchmal mögen sehn,
Was die und die, die an den Wallfahrtsort
Mit heiligen Gedanken kam,
Für fremde Mienen an sich nahm,
Wenn der verwegne Eremit
Fein listig, Schritt vor Schritt,
Vom Geist aufs Fleisch zu reden kam."

Of course the good women are shocked at first but they quickly succumb –

(1. 174 ff.) "Allein, dass die Versöhnung ausgeblieben,
Glaub ich und, wer die Weiber kennt,
Nicht eher, als kein Stroh mehr brennt."

The sense of pride and shame of these women is no more deep-seated than their piety, while the hermit, in spite of his show of Christian devotion, is a lascivious charlatan by whom an entire community permits itself to be seduced. He is a figure such as Lessing may have had in mind when he said, "Wenn der Teufel und ein Eremite lange beisammen leben, so wird entweder der Teufel ein Eremite, oder der Eremite ein Teufel werden" (*Lessings Werke, Bd. X, Nachlass,* p. 326).

The hermit manages to prolong his activities for well over a year. His infamy is finally disclosed to the judge by two girls who are jealous of their mothers – to comment upon such acid irony would be superfluous. When the hermit is brought before the court, the men of the community are ridiculed by the judge. The latter promises to mitigate the hermit's punishment if he will give the names of the ladies whom he has known. The judge is motivated solely by a sadistic desire to see his neighbors squirm in embarassment. He wrongly believes his own wife to be innocent, since she had paid only one visit to the "Waldseraph" –

(1. 264 ff.)   "Denk immer so, zu deiner Ruh,
            Lacht gleich die Wahrheit und der Dichter,
            Und deine fromme Frau dazu."

Prompted by the judge's insistence, however, the holy man reveals the piety and virtue of his wife also to be only illusory.

The poet suffixes a moral to his poem –

(1. 307, ff.)   "Wer seines Nächsten Schande sucht,
            Wird selber seine Schande finden!
            Nicht wahr, so liest man mich mit Frucht
            Und ich erzähle sonder Sünden?"

The purpose of the moral is ostensibly to transform the tale from a "Weibermärchen" (derived from the *Facetiae* of Poggio) to a respectable "Lehrgedicht." It is clear, nevertheless, that the moral is completely superfluous to the real essence of the poem, which is not to be found in the contemptible efforts of the judge to scandalize his townsmen. This moral seemingly shifts the weight of the poet's attack from the hermit and his devotees to the judge, by making the latter the subject of a joke.

The essence of the poem is rather in the attack upon false piety and the empty display of virtue; the hermit is the instrument of this attack. The weakness of the women of Kerapolis is typical of the sham Christianity which, put to the test, betrays a behaviour quite opposed to all pious pretenses. The hermit, himself, is the motivating personality of the tale. He is the very embodiment of hypocrisy through his pretense of holiness. Later, in the person of the Patriarch in *Nathan der Weise*, Lessing was to launch, from another angle, a much sharper and more serious attack on sham Christianity.

The objective delineation of the hermit figure in this early poem and the purpose for which it is used are quite typical of Lessing's "Aufklärung" attitude toward bigotry and hypocrisy in general. The poem satirizes human gullibility (and feminine frailty) in general, but it is quite specifically a Voltairean attack on church and priesthood. Lessing's stand is that of the seeker after truth and, as we have already suggested, the little poem represents a milestone in this particular direction of his thinking.

(2) In contrast to Lessing's iconoclastic rationalism, the advent of "Storm and Stress" conclusively placed the accent in German literature once more upon the expression of emotion and experience through feeling. Nature became a mirror of life, itself. Goethe's little drama, *Satyros*, presents a humorous conflict based upon two interpretations of nature as religion. The figure of the hermit is the protagonist of Goethe, himself, while Satyros, the antagonist, is, perhaps, the Herder of Goethe's Strassburg period (Max Morris, *Der junge Goethe*, Vol. 6, p. 309), disparaging toward the efforts of the young poet, yet expecting unwavering worship in return. On another level, the little comedy becomes a medium for Goethe's "Auseinandersetzung" with the more extreme aspects of "Storm and Stress". The hermit is the exponent of a true understanding of nature and Satyros is the false prophet of an exaggerated primitivism; he dupes the people into deifying him. Goethe's hermit, as opposed to Lessing's, is wronged and persecuted both by Satyros and by the misled Arcadian community.

In his opening speech, the hermit explains his reasons for deserting city life to dwell alone among the eternal beauties of nature. He has not removed himself from the city explicitly because of his distaste for the standards of behaviour there; indeed, the vanity of that life would have served to amuse him –

(1. 5-8) "Ich hab mich nicht hierher begeben,
Weil die in Städten so ruchlos leben
Und alle wandeln nach ihrem Trieb,
Der Schmeichler, Heuchler und der Dieb:
Das hätt mich immerfort ergetzt, –."

It is, rather, the arrogant and uncompromising attitude of these city-dwellers, which has driven him to the rich solace of nature; the city-dwellers demand unqualified respect precisely for their hypocrisy –

(1. 9 ff.) "Wollten sie nur nicht sein hochgeschätzt,
Bestehlen und be – mich wie die Raben,
Und noch dazu Reverenzen haben!
Ihrer langweiligen Narrheit satt,
Bin herausgezogen in Gottes Stadt, –."

This hermit perceives nature as a representation of life in all its myriad activity, as a cosmos. Nature is, to him, "Gottes Stadt", full of living images of fertility, of continuous creation and recreation ("Werden"). The verses given here to the hermit constitute an early exposition of Goethe's "Naturanschauung" – and one of his most charming expressions of it. Nature is not the booty of Philistines ("der steif Philister") to be trammeled and violated for the course pleasure of base tastes.

The hermit sees the blossoms and buds of spring, the promise of plenty. He describes the activity of the smallest of creatures, each a moving, creating, developing glint in the mosaic of nature –

(1. 26 ff.) "Da lockt uns denn der Sonnenschein,
Storch und Schwalb aus der Fremd herein,
Den Schmetterling aus seinem Haus,
Die Fliegen aus den Ritzen raus
Und brütet das Raupenvölklein.
Das quillt all von Erzeugungskraft,
Wie sich's hat aus dem Schlaf gerafft;
Vogel und Frosch und Tier und Mücken
Begehn sich zu allen Augenblicken,
Hinten und vorn, auf Bauch und Rücken,
Dass man auf jeder Blüt und Blatt
Ein Eh – und Wochenbettlein hat.
Und sing ich dann im Herzen mein
Lob Gott mit allen Würmelein –."

That is the pulsing, kaleidoscopic world, endlessly recreating itself, which the hermit has made his own. It is, we may say, the basis of his religion, for all of it reveals a sense of eternal purpose. In these surroundings the hermit lives in peace, tending his garden and fruits, and protecting them from frost, caterpillars, and the dry heat of summer. Outwardly he presents a traditional conception of the recluse. The inward experiencing of nature depicted above, however, is new, profound, and typical of Goethe. It is the hermit's world of nature, his religion, which is opposed by that of Satyros, who embodies much of the exaggeration which was present in "Storm and Stress" thinking and writing.

The hermit acts fully in accordance with his mode of life when he takes the injured Satyros into his hut, for it was customary, as we have seen (Introduction), for the recluse to offer hospitality and aid to those in need of it. The animal qualities which motivate Satyros' lust (not love) for the natural life are suggested by his agonized howling outside the hut. The hermit supposes it to be that of some wounded beast. The absolute lack of any ground for basic understanding between Satyros and the hermit is made clear by the thankless, arrogant behaviour of the former (1. 60-71 ff.). Satyros criticizes the poverty and simplicity of the good hermit's household; he demands wine and fruit, and is indignant at the hermit's offer of milk and bread. The bestial character of Satyros and his interpretation of nature as an element to be plundered for the satisfaction of his own ego illustrate an attitude toward the world strongly opposed to the deeply natural harmony in which the hermit lives.

Satyros calls the abode of the hermit a "Hundelagerstatt" and "ein's Missetäters Folterbett". Left alone to rest by the hermit, the point-eared villain gives vent to the contempt in which he holds his benefactor. His feelings reveal in exaggerated form the "Storm and Stress" desire to revolt against accepted traditions. Here Satyros shows his distaste for the symbolic object of the hermit's devotion –

(1. 103 ff.) "Da ist dem Kerl sein Platz zu beten.
 Es tut mir in den Augen weh,
 Wenn ich dem Narren seinen Herrgott seh!"

Satyros would rather set in place of the hermit's crucifix an onion. He would substitute a tangible (and edible) symbol of nature which he cen grasp for one which signifies a power greater than his, and which is therefore incomprehensible to him –

(1. 106 ff.) "Wollt lieber eine Zwiebel anbeten,
 Bis mir die Thrän in die Augen träten,
 Als öffnen meines Herzens Schrein
 Einem Schnitzbildlein, Querhölzelein.
 Mir geht in der Welt nichts über mich:
 Denn Gott ist Gott, und ich bin ich."

He steals a cloth from the hermit to cover his wild nakedness from any maidens he may encounter, hurls the crucifix into the river (revolt against the order worshipped by the hermit), and stealthily sneaks off.

Satyros pours all the seductive power of spring into his song at the well (1. 134 ff.), and it embodies the fertile drive of procreating nature which was expressed in the hermit's opening monologue. Satyros' song, however, stresses the sultry, intangibly sensuous aspect of it. The spell of his music and his animal impetuosity enchant the naive, innocent Psyche; only Arsinoe (and later her mother, Eudora) is shrewd enough to perceive Satyros for what he is –

(1. 148 ff.) *Psyche*
"Welch göttlich hohes Angesicht!

Arsinoe
Siehst denn seine langen Ohren nicht?"

Just as the force of his animal passion overcomes Psyche, so the power of Satyros' speech and the wildness of his appearance impress the people who follow Hermes and his daughter, Arsinoe, to see the strange nature god. Satyros wishes them to discard their unnatural clothing and to cease acting as slaves to custom. They are to emerge from the imprisonment of their houses, and live as in the golden age of natural man. Trees will be their tents, the grass their carpet, and raw chestnuts their food –
(1. 274)   "Und rohe Kastanien ein herrlicher Frass –!"
The crowd, moved, but not grasping the sense of the speech (a take-off on Rousseau's cult of "raw nature"), seizes upon the only tangible prospect which comes to the surface of Satyros' torrent of words – raw chestnuts. Then, completely overwhelmed by his turbulent delineation of the creation, the gullible people proclaim the half-animal to be their god (1. 288-316).

When the good hermit appears, and accosts his erstwhile guest as an ill-tempered, disgraceful beast, the two exponents of nature stand face to face. The hermit, as we have seen, sees nature as the revelation of God's ceaseless creation and inviolate order, while Satyros, the hypocritical god of bestial feeling, conceives of all nature as the nourishment of his ego –

(1. 169 ff.)   "Mein ist die ganze weite Welt,
                Ich wohne, wo mir's wohl gefällt;
                Ich herrsch übers Wild und Vogelheer,
                Frucht auf der Erden und Fisch im Meer."

The thoroughly impetuous behaviour of the people illustrates the danger of unrestrained feeling and its effect upon a mass personality. In a state of blind irrationality, into which Satyros has led them, they wish to put the hermit to death for blasphemy against their newfound god. The hermit is saved by Hermes' wife, the clear-sighted Eudora, who tempts Satyros into the temple. As soon as her cries are heard, Hermes and his fellowers discover Satyros attempting to embrace her; only then do they clearly see their god as the beast he actually is.

The hermit with his deep insight into nature is misunderstood by the people as a group; Eudora, alone, in whose house he is imprisoned, sympathizes with him and distinguishes between the truth of his way of life and that of Satyros –

(1. 373)   "Dich um des Tiers Willen töten!"

The hermit, however, is resigned to his fate, for he knows well the ways of life and the world –

(1. 370 ff.)   "Sie glauben. Lass sie! Du wirst nichts gewinnen.
           Das Schicksal spielt
           Mit unsrem armen Kopf und Sinnen."

In his resignation, he is prepared to pardon the society which persecutes him; he recognizes in the behavior of the people the same desire to comprehend life which in him has been fulfilled –

(1. 374 ff.)   "Wer sein Herz bedürftig fühlt,
           Findt überall einen Propheten."

Unlike Lessing's hypocritical "Eremit" who plays upon the false piety and weakness of the citizens of Kerapolis, Goethe's hermit is persecuted by a deluded society in the throes of a nature "Schwärmerei". Goethe's recluse has discovered the deep truths of life in nature to which the people have been blinded by the very heat of their desire to find them – Goethe's little farce has serious, often tragic undertones.

When death seems inevitable to him, the hermit has only one specific regret. He has lived for one purpose, to acquire the deep knowledge of nature which he now possesses, and, perhaps, to pass it on to a happier race of men –

(1. 438 ff.)   "Doch *das* schmerzt mich nur,
           Dass ich die tiefe Kenntnis der Natur
           Mit Müh geforscht und leider! nun vergebens;
           Dass hohe Menschenwissenschaft
           Manche geheimnisvolle Kraft
           Mit diesem Geist der Erd entschwinden soll."

This hermit would wish to teach each of the people, individually, some single bit of the profound knowledge which he has absorbed (1. 447-450). His insight into nature is an individual experience acquired through a refinement of the senses to the creative harmony round about him. The truth of life, as he knows it, cannot be massexperienced; the mass drunkenness of feeling which Satyros arouses in the people as a whole is an illusory religion. The hermit expresses this, when he says –

(1. 448 ff.)   "Ich wollte jeden sein eigen Kunststück lehren,
           Einen jeden eins:
           Denn was alle wissen, ist keins.–

Thus Goethe's solitary very nearly becomes a martyr for his individual belief which is incomprehensible to the people as a whole. The material of conflict in the play, as we have said, is the incompatibility between two concepts of nature as religion. The hermit reveals in his personality the deep insight into divine order which is the fruit of inward intimate experience ("Erlebnis"); Satyros represents the violently exaggerated emotionalism ("Masslosigkeit") of more conventional "Storm and Stress", which has its most direct effect collectively. The hermit's conception of nature is a revelation of eternal harmony, while Satyros' animal turbulence is a travesty on divine order. (This conflict also very clearly points to Goethe's own subjugation of the more extreme elements of "Storm and Stress" in himself.)

Several characteristics and themes associated with this hermit figure are especially noteworthy. The hermit in *Satyros* is (unlike Lessing's, but more like Trevrizent or Simplicissimus) a carefully drawn individual personality – not merely a type. (He is a self-portrait of young Goethe on the side of his fervent adoration of nature.) He embodies the profound conception of nature as a creative cosmos, a revelation of eternal harmony of which he, as an individual, is an integral part. We have also observed his desire to impart some of this knowledge to his fellow-men (as in *Hyperion*, where, however, the theme is the development of the hero's conception of nature and the awareness of his particular relationship to it). To be emphasized most strongly is the fact that the hermit experiences nature specifically as "Gottes Stadt", which suggests that its intricate processes reveal the purpose of a divine will and the eternally harmonious design of life. This interpretation of nature by Goethe's hermit is of the utmost importance as a theme which is developed (and differentiated, of course) in connection with many other figures in this and the following chapters (in spite of the distinguishing chapter-headings).

The hermit's relationship to society is developed on two levels in *Satyros*. First, in the exposition of the opening monologue, the hermit explains that he has abandoned life in the city because of the hypocritical demands made upon him. To find the true essence of life he has gone to nature. Second, the substance of the drama, itself, involves a conflict between two interpretations of nature as religion. That of the hermit is based upon deep personal experience of a specifically individual kind which cannot readily be imparted to the people collectively. That which is imparted by Satyros, on the other hand, is based upon an irrationally emotional reaction of the people as a whole; it readily alleviates the natural desire for an understanding of life through nature without supplying any deeper truth or personal conviction – mass hypnotism, rather than enlightenment. Consequently, the people, deluded and confused by Satyros, are prepared to martyr the hermit, whose conception of life is inaccessible through any process other than that of individual experience ("Erlebnis").

(3) Because of the fragmentary form in which it has come down to us, Lenz's *Die Kleinen* presents certain limitations to the analysis of themes and characters. Yet we are justified in believing that the major ones stand before us in the six scenes which Lenz actually executed, as well as in the sketches which he drew of intermediary and (apparently) final scenes. There is enough to reveal plainly the subject matter and the backbones of the two connected plots in which it is treated.

The material of the first plot is an essentially typical one for "Storm and Stress" writing; it is the theme of revolt against the upper classes and an expression of contempt for the over-refinement, decadence, and lack of genuine humanity in the life of such circles. Contrasted with the characteristics of the aristocracy are the sincere and earthy virtues of the peasant and serving classes.

The central figure is Hanns von Engelbrecht, who has become sadly disillusioned in his own social stratum; therefore he sets out to observe the lower classes. He wishes to find his happiness by feeling that of others and by making them aware of their more fortunate lot (as in *Werther* – Lenz was, of course, an avid disciple of Goethe and strove to emulate him in his life and work).

The second plot is connected technically with the first through the central character, Engelbrecht. Here, the sad conflict between the hermit and his older brother (the "Bruderzwist" – another popular "Sturm und Drang" theme) and the hermit's complete despair in the later scenes portray the tragic fate which befalls two men in the treacherous spider-web of court intrigue. This second plot has a more truly dramatic nature than do the scenes of the first, which depict the loves and activities of "Die Kleinen". The lives of "Die Kleinen" do provide vivid and lively portrayals, but they are episodic – more like background studies against which the theme specifically involving the hermit, Bismark, and Engelbrecht stands out in bold relief.

We have called Engelbrecht the central character of the fragment, but this is so technically rather than intrinsically. The hermit and Bismark (and all of the vividly drawn characters of the lower class scenes) are vastly more interesting and important than Engelbrecht, himself. He is used by the poet to provide the human meeting ground of experience which sets off the naive and happier lives of Annamarie and her "Schlossergesell" or of Lorchen, the chambermaid, and the hunter, Hummel, from the tragedy of the hermit and his brother.

The second scene introduces the hermit, whom Engelbrecht encounters sitting before his cave with his face half turned toward its entrance as if in painful disdain of the world. He appears to live in the traditional manner of the hermits discussed in all of the previous works. He dwells in a cave upon a mountain-side, and lives on roots and herbs. Like Trevrizent, he is an experienced venerable man who has secluded himself from the world for many years – (p. 318) "Lieber Jüngling, kommt Ihr, nach fünfzig Jahren meine eingetrockneten Augen wieder einmal anzufeuchten?" The hermit's behaviour throughout the scene discloses the deep despair which the world has inflicted upon him. Engelbrecht hears no logical explanation for this sorrow, but he needs none; general remarks, even hints suffice for him. Feeling and emotion are the touchstones of relationship and Engelbrecht and the hermit need only to sense the force and direction of each other's emotional reactions to understand one another completely.

When asked for a simple direction, the hermit makes clear the state of utter rejection of the world in which he exists. He does not even reply, but simply points out the path with his finger. His rejoinder to Engelbrecht's query as to whether he is a Carthusian – "Nein – lebt wohl, mein Herr.!" – shows his adamant desire to avoid any involvement with his fellow-men or the world outside. In this respect, he displays a streak of the pathological fear and distrust of the world which we have seen in *Simplicissimus* (and which we shall observe in Peter Schlemihl). He does not exhibit any natural sense of hospitality such as that of Trevrizent or of Goethe's recluse.

Engelbrecht, nevertheless, immediately understands the aged man – (p. 317) "Was hat Euch die Welt so verhasst gemacht?" The hermit's response ("die Welt") overwhelms Engelbrecht, who kisses the old man's hand as if he were a saint. This token of deep understanding and sympathy causes the hermit remorse, and through Engelbrecht he feels again a bond of kinship with mankind – (p. 318) "Jüngling, Ihr schenkt mir das Leben wieder!" The tremendous force of the hermit's revulsion from the world, the very scope of his emotion, we might say, convinces the younger man that a figure of greatness stands before him who, but for the fateful cause of his despair, may have been destined to play a most important role in life. The hermit, however, designates his solitary existence as precisely the great role he has been fated to perform. This sentiment is echoed by Engelbrecht when he takes leave of the recluse – (p. 319) "O ich möchte verstummen wie du! Heiliger grosser göttlicher Mann! Dass deine Füsse die Erde berühren, die sich unter ihnen verächtlich dahinrollt! Wer soll dich schätzen, wenn du dich nicht schätzest? Du, wie Gott, dir selber genug, dir selber Belohnung, dir selber alles!" In these lines the hermit is made to represent the revolt of the almost divine individual against a defective world.

The hermit informs Engelbrecht that he has fled in order to leave open the way for his closest friend's worldly success. To save that friend from becoming guilty of treachery and machination against him – as Heidemann later hints, (p. 325) and to preserve the ideal of a friendship which could not have endured in a society motivated by intrigue and favoritism, the great man removed himself to the wilds.

The nature of his withdrawal, therefore, proves to be that of a self-sacrifice to save a friend (his brother, as is subsequently revealed). In this respect, his act also shows a strong relationship to that of Trevrizent. Trevrizent, however, rejected a knightly world in which he strongly believed, while Lenz's hermit casts off a society which, because of its decadence, endangers an ideal. Lenz's figure also contrasts with the hermit in *Satyros*, where a susceptible society is victimized by the satyr, but is considered by the hermit worthy and capable of development because of its natural urge to discover the essence of life. The theme of martyrdom and holiness is suggested in Trevrizent, and is strong in both *Satyros* and *Die Kleinen*.

Lenz's hermit desires that knowledge of his sacrifice be withheld from all men; Engelbrecht is the first man with whom he has spoken since his hermithood and he is to be the last. Having shut himself completely off from the world, he feels the frost of death creeping through his bones, and this sense of foreboding suggests the chilling atmosphere of despair in which the hermit ends his life.

Having received an invitation from Count Bismark (the hermit's brother), Engelbrecht stops at an inn to inquire the way to the nobleman's country estate. Here he discovers from the innkeeper, Heidemann, a good deal about the past lives of the two brothers. From Heidemann's description of the Count, Engelbrecht gains the information which the hermit had denied him – namely that Count Bismark is the friend and brother for whom the hermit had abandoned life in society. From the common rumors which Heidemann passes on to him, Engelbrecht receives the impression that the Count's success at the prince's court was shortlived. The hermit's sacrifice seems to have been in vain. We find this confirmed in the subsequent interview between Engelbrecht and Bismark.

As prime minister, Bismark soon discovered that he was falling out of favor with the prince, whereupon he immediately withdrew to a lonely country estate. There he lives in deepest melancholy – in contrast to the previous high spirits for which he had been noted (p. 325). Some rumors attribute this depression to the death of Bismark's daughter. Others maintain that it is because of a younger brother who had been the prince's favorite, but whom Bismark so maligned that he fled to the wilds. Engelbrecht learns that the younger Bismark had been a dashing and successful officer in the prince's bodyguard. In a battle he had lost two fingers, and had received a scar on the face. These details identify the hermit for Engelbrecht.

This certainty as to the hermit's identity ripens the young man's resolution to bring the two brothers together — to effect a reconciliation which might relieve the tortured conscience of Count Bismark and win the hermit recognition for his heart-breaking sacrifice.

Bismark, when he receives Engelbrecht, appears as a broken man in the depths of a melancholy which is the wage and fruit of his intrigue at court. Curious and fascinated by his visitor's project to observe the virtuous happiness of the lower classes, the Count eagerly scans Engelbrecht's writing portfolio. His glance falls at once upon the entry concerning the hermit. When Engelbrecht snatches the portfolio from him to keep his oath of secrecy to the hermit, the Count's remark (p. 335) — "Wenn das ist — Ich weiss was Meineid ist. — Lasst mich!" indicates the source of his suffering. His subsequent monologue in the garden discloses the pact which he, a hopeless weakling, had made with his brother. The younger brother was to absent himself from court and leave the field clear for the Count, after which the latter would care for his needs. This bargain took the form of an oath which the Count has not fulfilled. Lenz's portrait of Bismark is that of a weak aristrocat who succumbs to the decadent brilliance of court life, and uses the sacrifice of a noble brother to gain his end. Having fallen into disfavor, he suffers in solitude because it is too late to make good the broken oath or repay his brother's too generous love.

In the two final fragmentary monologues of the hermit (p. 337) and in the scene following them, Lenz's recluse takes on a pronouncedly pathological coloring. In the scene discussed earlier (Scene II), his complete and adamant rejection of society was delineated by his every gesture and word, but we have also noted that the sympathy and understanding of Engelbrecht evoked in him a natural longing for some bond with his fellow-men, while, at the same time, he voiced a wish to have the soundness of his reason established after his death (p. 319 — "Wenn ich tot bin, könnt Ihr meinen Namen in einen Stein schneiden, und denen, die mich für närrisch oder abergläubisch hielten, sagen, dass ich meinen gesunden Verstand hatte, wie sie"). We may imagine these desires to have been always present below the surface. The harsh disappointment occasioned by the experience with his brother, the Count, however, had called up in him an extreme revulsion for a society so decadent as to provide temptation for one brother to intrigue against the other for the sake of obtaining rank and favor. The hermit, Heinrich Bismark, had detected in his brother's character a weakness common to the aristocratic court circle as he knew it. To prevent his brother, therefore, from becoming guilty of intrigue against him, Heinrich became a hermit. His experience had embittered him to the extent that not only the scene of his former glory, but all human society had become distasteful to him.

In the first of the two final monologues (p. 337), the hermit expresses a horrible doubt as to the justification of his flight. It is clear that he is in a pathological state of mind. The greatness of his purpose no longer suffices to comfort him. The desire to have the soundness of his reason attested by Engelbrecht after his death has grown to exaggerated proportions – (p. 337) "Wem scheint nicht mein Leben eine Karikatur? Wenn wird der gütige Genius – niemals wird er erwachen, der ein wohltätiges Licht darauf wirft."

The hermit now feels that his very salvation depends upon the validity and justification of his withdrawal. His speech has the tone of a despairing attempt at self-persuasion; he maintains that he would repeat his actions even if they now be undone. His sole consolation consists in having caused no one unhappiness, for he has blocked no man's path to success. Yet this consolation does not ring true in his innermost soul, as he suggests in the exclamation, "Guter Gott! erhalte mir das Gefühl in der Todesstunde!"

In the opening words of the second monologue ("kurz vor seinem Tode im letzten Akt"), the hermit apostrophizes the impotent thinking which has led him astray like a will-o'-the-wisp in the marshes. He is referring directly to the wishful thinking which lets him console himself with the idea that his brother's happiness is well worth the sacrificial withdrawal from the world. His soul is torn apart by the horrible doubt which possesses him – "Der du meine Seele geschaffen hast, rette mich – meine Seele so kalt und gross, so unleidenschaftlich für meinen verzweifelten Schmerz – so eine Kotseele für mein Elend!" He feels incapable ot coping with his despair – despair growing out of the reality which would not have permitted him to forsake the world to gratify a decadent and weakling brother. The pathological emotion of the hermit is evident in the last attempt to persuade himself that his long life as a recluse has not been in vain – "und doch freut es mich einen Bruder damit glücklich gemacht zu haben, einen Bruder, der feuriger als ich, sein Elend so kalten Bluts wie ich nicht ertragen haben würde. Und wohl elend hätte er müssen sein, weil aus Furcht vor diesem Zustande er mich hilflos gelassen."

Then the pangs of approaching death come upon him – "meine Brust hebt sich, ungewöhnliche Zuckungen, Leiden, die ich noch nie erfahren, folgen blitzschnell aufeinander" – and in this state of supersensitivity he feels the judgment of God (and in this respect

Lenz's hermit is also traditionally Christian). Lying prostrate, the hermit believes that he has been rejected, because his action was based upon a false generosity. He had no right to leave his brother alone on the political and social stage. He, himself, might have been of greater service to the world; it was his duty to oppose the designs of the decadent weakling, not to flee from them. Thus, the despairing thought which plagues his last moments becomes crushing reality – "O Gedanke, der die ganze Hölle in sich führt, verfolgst du mich so spät – am Ende der Laufbahn? – Verfehlt – ein ganzes langes Patriarchenleben – und mein Tod – unbekannt – unberühmt – unwürdig!"

After the hermit's terrible struggle with his soul and the hopeless impact of its outcome, the scene which follows it is anticlimactic, but it does fulfill the poet's intention of reuniting the two brothers through Engelbrecht. Of particular interest is the hermit's expression of joy when Engelbrecht and Count Bismark make their way to him through driving snow and icy wind – (p. 339) "und es ist etwas süsses, deinem Ende in Gesellschaft von Menschen entgegengehen. Ich habe in meinem Leben die Menschen gemieden, nur für das letzte Viertelstündchen habe ich mir einen Zuschauer gewünscht – mein Gebet ist erhört." The sense of well-being derived from human society about him in his last moments is based upon the final realization (as we have seen) that the motive for his hermithood was not valid – which does not mean that he now feels differently about the vanity and decadence of the aristocratic world and its "Ruhmsucht", but that his flight actually meant a neglect of duty.

When Heinrich, with his last breath, stretches out his arms to the Count, we must interpret the gesture as one of forgiveness. He feels that he bears the responsibility not only for his own, but also for whatever misery the weaker man has endured; for he had abandoned him with full knowledge of that weakness. The Count stabs himself and falls beside the body of the hermit brother who had rejected the world and sacrificed his life for his sake in vain.

In a sense, the figure of the hermit, Heinrich Bismark, expresses a sort of repudiation of hermithood, for he deceives himself into rejecting the world through partial weakness of character. As we have indicated, the decadence of the upper classes as opposed to the simple virtues of "die Kleinen" is the dominant theme of the fragment. The conflict between the hermit and his brother illustrates the devastating effect of the former way of life upon two individuals caught in its web of intrigue. The weakness of the Count ruins the life of a stronger, nobler brother who thus falls prey to the same decadent order. We might say that Count Bismark embodies the aristocratic decadence because of which the hermit rejected the world to spend his remaining years in solitude – although in vain.

The words of Engelbrecht spoken over the brothers' bodies form a kind of epilogue – "O schreckliches Schauspiel! Eitle Grösse! O fürchterliches Ziel der mühsamen Laufbahn! Wohin, Hochmut, auf welche Klippen führst du uns? – Sie sterben und ich bleibe, ihre Körper zu vereinigen. O ihr Himmlischen, verlasst meine Seele nicht, wenn sie je sich auf ähnliche Abwege verirren wollte!"

The theme of martyrdom is suggested by Trevrizent's withdrawal to atone for his brother's sin, but the theme is decidedly strong in Goethe's *Satyros*. Heinrich Bismark, however, in Lenz's fragment becomes a martyr to the effeteness and sterile lust for worldly brilliance in aristocratic society. Lenz's hermit falls victim to the very decadence and intrigue which he seeks to avoid, for, in removing himself from the path of the weaker brother's success, he capitulates to that very weakness. He deceives himself into believing that he has acted out of generosity, whereas his flight actually represented a lack of strength in his own character. The valid and true revolt, however, would have consisted in standing firm against the decadence and corruption round about; thus he might have performed a valuable service to the world. Lenz's hermit, therefore, becomes the principal actor in a tragedy of revolt against an aristocracy of intrigue and corruption.

In contrast to Trevrizent, whose act consists of atonement for a sin against the ideal society in which he has the utmost faith, and in contrast, also, with Goethe's hermit, who understands the motives of society about him, and has a sympathetic attitude toward it, Lenz's figure illustrates an unsuccessful revolt against a specific class of society. His whole being is repelled by its "unnaturalness".

Goethe's hermit has the profound world of nature, "Gottes Stadt", which he can substitute for that which he left. Lenz's hermit has no substitute in nature, but only his great soul – and he almost compromises its salvation. The role of nature, itself, as opposed to the superficialities of society, is not stressed in *Die Kleinen* as it is in *Satyros* or in Klinger's *Sturm und Drang*. The icy wind and snow flurries in the scene last discussed are used to suggest an atmosphere of doom and hopelessness descriptive of the hermit's state of mind. Lenz does, however, introduce the concept of an individual with natural, therefore noble instincts into his portrayal of the hermit. The pathological element is injected into the hermit's struggle with his soul and the attempt is made successfully in *Die Kleinen* to give the hermit tragic stature. As a ruler with which the faults of a class and period are measured (true also of Goethe's recluse and Lessing's), the hermit in *Die Kleinen* illustrates specifically the unsuccessful revolt of a strong individual against a class of society so corrupt that even he cannot prevail against its influences – there is a sense of hopelessness which borders on nihilism in the portrayal of Heinrich Bismark.

(4) In contrast to Lenz's fragment, Klinger's drama, *Sturm und Drang*, does not contain such a violent attack against any specific class of society, but it does criticize superficiality of feeling principally through the character of Blasius (there is also much satirizing of the Anacreontic view of life as embodied in the characters of La Feu and Lady Katherine). Feeling above all else is exalted; indeed, the play possesses (and often chastises) in exaggerated form all the stylistic mannerisms of the movement to which it gave its name. In it we can expect no logical development of motives, but must penetrate through the emotional expressions to arrive at any systematic understanding.

Of the characters as such, Blasius ("der Blasius", a blasé person) is drawn with most depth. Although Blasius does not appear as a hermit technically in the drama, he does, nevertheless, decide to reject the world (Act V, Scene 4) in order to become one. What is important is the fact that he reveals an attitude of disillusionment, even of disgust, toward the world, and we are given a picture of the relationship to society which brings him to substitute for its superficialities (like the hermit in *Satyros*) the deeper eternal world of nature. We have, in other words, before us the development of thought and feeling which ends in Blasius' hermithood, while, in the previous works, we have looked through the recluse into his past, as it were, to evaluate his present.

Blasius holds a position in the drama which is midway between the stormy, impulsive activity of Wild and the unbridled, imaginative flights of La Feu into his pastoral paradise. When the play opens in an American inn during the revolution, the three comrades sound the respective key-notes of their personalities. Wild had whisked his friends willy-nilly from Russia to Spain and thence to the promised land of individual freedom and revolt against tyranny. He revels in the excitement and turmoil; paradoxically, the uproar of the revolutionary atmosphere is supposed to relax and free his innermost self – (*Deutsche National-Literatur, Stürmer und Dränger I*, I, 1, p. 65) "Das wilde Geräusch hat mir schon soviel Wohlsein entgegen gebrüllt, dass mirs wirklich ein wenig anfängt besser zu werden. Soviel hundert Meilen gereiset, um dich in vergessenden Lärmen zu bringen – Tolles Herz! du sollst mirs danken! Ha! tobe und spanne dich dann aus, labe dich im Wirrwarr!" Wild, of course, seeks solace because he has been separated from his childhood beloved, Karoline Berkley, by the emnity of their respective fathers, the Lords Buschy and Berkley.

La Feu's tempestuous activity (if it may be so designated) consists, on the other hand, of creating the most fantastic illusions for the edification and stimulation of his senses – (I, 1 – p. 65) "Es lebe die Illusion! – Ei! Ei!, Zauber meiner Phantasie, wandle in den Rosengarten von Phyllis Hand geführt –". Subsequent elaborations of this theme emphasize to what extent Klinger lets La Feu carry his imagination which corresponds in its paradoxical workings to Wild's means of seeking consolation – (I, 1 – p. 65) "Beim Amor! ich will mich wie ein alt Weib verlieben, in einem alten, baufälligen Haus wohnen, meinen zarten Leib in stinkenden Mistlaken baden, bloss um meine Phantasie zu scheren. Ist keine alte Hexe da, mit der ich scharmieren könnte?"

Between these two figures stands Blasius, who is tired of the world's superficialities. He has no taste for their excesses. To them, he is "lieber, bissiger, kranker Blasius."

Although he maintains that he loves nothing, Blasius does love the world – but for its own sake and not for the excesses and trivialities which make a travesty of life in it.

We become aware that his relationships with women have much to do with his depressed state of mind and his attitude toward society, for they have, with one exception, been unfortunate. The recurring concern for Donna Isabella ("Kommt meine Donna noch?" and "Ist Donna Isabella noch?") permits the conclusion that Blasius had experienced through her the one deep love of his life – (I, 1 – p. 67) "In Krieg und Getümmel von meiner Passion weg, das Einzige was mir übrig blieb." Blasius had known her in Spain and his temporary resentment toward Wild is partially due to his having been wrenched from her against his will. This experience, however, is only one of the immediate causes of the melancholy which pervades his outlook upon life.

The level of his feeling is not always comprehensible to his friends because of its depth. When Wild says, (I, 1 – p. 67) "Du liebst ja nichts, Blasius," the reply is taken only at an apparent surface value. Blasius answers that he loves nothing, that he has consciously brought himself to a point where he loves nothing – that is, to love everything and to forget it all again in the very same moment. In reality, his attitude is one of self-protection; he wishes to preserve his sincere and sensitive heart from further pain and disappointment. This is the motive which underlies his frequent expressions of negation and his general behaviour in the drama; it is essentially the motive which prompts him finally to seek seclusion in nature.

Blasius would betray all women, he maintains, and in return they would betray, and have betrayed him. To his own disgust he has played the social game – acted as fop and as stormy young petrel, as dullard and as hypersensitive personality, according to the demands of the moment. His only conquest was that of Donna Isabella, because he pretended to be nothing other than himself.

Human relationship, as he observes it, is based upon triviality, sham, and illusion, and society, for him, is inhabited by shallow personalities only.

Despite the fact that Wild's desire for strenuous activity oppresses him (II, 1 – end), Blasius also longs for the zest in life which his friend displays. The unhappy man suffers from a neurotic strain which has been nurtured in him by his experiences in the world – (II, 1 – end) "Ich bin zerrissen in mir und kann die Fäden nicht wieder auffinden das Leben anzuknüpfen." Implicit in this self-examination is the desire to construct a shell around his own sensitivity and, on the other hand, the natural drive to find an emotional outlet for himself. He recalls the painful occasion (witnessed by Wild) when he was forced to see his charger put to use as a drayhorse. The depressing sight caused him to weep, and Isabella, understanding his emotion, wiped his tears away. This incident has a symbolic value for Blasius; it illustrates, very simply, the deterioration of the joy which he once did have in life. He is now, as we have seen, completely disillusioned – (II, 1 – end) "Herrlichkeit der Welt! Ich kann keine deiner Blumen mehr brechen. Ja, wer diesen Sinn verloren hat, wer dich verloren hat, ewige Liebe, die du in uns alles zusammen hältst!" In these lines, Blasius infers that he has lost the sense of communion with the world (a sense similar to that which does inspire Goethe's hermit in *Satyros*), but the tone of the lines also conveys an unexpressed wish, a desire to find some realm of life in which his suppressed longing may find its release.

We have already suggested that Blasius' past relationships with women make up a principal cause for his melancholy attitude and distaste for society. With the single exception of Donna Isabella, the women in his life have embodied the triviality and general emptiness of all social intercourse. It is safe to assume that the resulting disillusionment has colored his entire approach to life; he had presumably sought release for his inner self through his relationships with the opposite sex. Having been disappointed and deeply hurt, he attempts to shield himself from the world by closing off his emotion. Yet, as we have also seen, the drive to feel life in all its fullness still pulses strongly in him – albeit hidden beneath a negativistic exterior.

Women have been largely responsible for Blasius' disillusionment. Through them, society has become a threat to his sincere and deep emotion; he feels he must protect himself from the superficiality which directs the course of human relationships. Yet, the conscious attempt to close himself off emotionally from the world discloses the underlying drive in Blasius to find release for his feelings – to reestablish the bonds severed between himself and life.

Blasius' longing reaches its final solution through his experience with Luise. She embodies conclusively for him all of the superficial contradictions which have produced his negative attitude toward life. This final experience with the superficially Rococo feminine personality provides the impulse which causes Blasius to reject all human society. He finds release from the pain of a sham existence and rediscovers the "Herrlichkeit der Welt" in the revelation of cosmic nature – in it he achieves at last a feeling of complete harmony. This solution is prepared for Blasius by the contrast which is implicit in the natural beauty of Luise and her emotional artificiality and emptiness. She is almost programmatic for his dualistic approach to life. In addition, her superficiality oppresses his natural longing, and contrasts with the pulsation of nature embodied in a magnificent evening which does speak to Blasius' demand for deep emotional harmony.

The disappointment resulting from this encounter with Luise calls up in Blasius all of his resentment toward the lack of true feeling which stamps the creatures of social tradition.

While walking with Luise, La Feu, and Kathrin, Blasius becomes so depressed that he refuses to continue the stroll. In Luise's company, the evening seems wet and cold. Following the walk, La Feu and Blasius sit alone in the garden (IV, 6), and, in the magic stillness of the night air, the earlier dampness and cold is no longer apparent. Instead, particularly to Blasius, the encompassing aspect of night becomes charged with emotional life of its own. Nature reveals itself cloaked in the mantle of night as a living cosmic organism – the source and receptacle of all deep feeling. A response from the harmony of which he now feels himself to be part speaks mightily to the pent-up longing in Blasius' soul. After previously having plunged to the utmost depth of depression, he finds an ecstatic release. His emotion, turned inward by the unnatural Luise, bursts its corporal limits, and becomes an overtone in the pervading chord of nature, itself.

This brief scene (IV, 6) represents the fulfillment of Blasius' destiny in the drama, and characterizes his transition to hermithood. While La Feu and Wild find self-realization in the loves of Kathrin and Karoline, respectively, Blasius turns from the oppressive superficiality of society to the living spirit of nature. This development is the climax of his life. The ecstasy expressed by Blasius to cosmic nature as revealed in night is very like that of Werther in the famous second letter "Am 10. Mai" – only there, of course, nature is clothed in the splendor of a spring morning. This conception of nature and night points to the related one of Novalis and his early romantic contemporaries. Blasius becomes fully conscious that, in the harmony of nature, he has found peace at last. His life has been a pilgrimage over ways beset with both joys and thorns to this end. He recalls once again his past life and the suffering he has endured from an insensitive world because it was his lot to be endowed with a feeling heart. Now, however, his deep emotion finds a positive response – "liebliche Lüfte gebt mir Liebe noch!"

In his last meeting with Luise (V, 4), Blasius makes a final attempt to discover in her some basis for compatibility (cf. IV, 6) but the revelation of nature which he has just experienced renders him quite sarcastic in his approach. Luise, shallow as she is, naturally does not comprehend the tone in Blasius' sarcastic proposal of marriage. They are admirably suited to one another, he finds, for they are both bored to death in each other's company. To be able to endure such a relationship is the primary requisite of marriage. Luise insists upon retorting to him and Blasius finds, as before, that she thus destroys whatever aura of attraction she may have possessed.

When La Feu and Kathrin agree to pass on into their imaginary "Schäferleben" together, Blasius announces his decision to become a hermit (V, 4). He has found a pleasant bushy cave where he can seclude himself from the society which has caused him so much pain. There he will preserve the feeling which still remains to him, and begin life anew in the harmony of nature – the life they had left behind in the Alps. (cf. Kleist's *Schweizer Idyll*).

We have seen that Blasius stands between La Feu with his Anacreontic flights of imagination and the tempestuous Wild. In him, Klinger clearly wishes to portray the conflict of deep (genuine "Sturm und Drang") feeling with the capricious superficiality of society, which is embodied, not only in society as a whole, but specifically in women such as Luise. The most typical "Sturm und Drang" characteristic, here, is the treatment of the unspecific quality, "Gefühl", for its own sake. Blasius, as a hermit, seeks seclusion in nature from the studied shallowness of society; his refuge in nature saves him from complete emotional paralysis – where, in *Simplicissimus*, the hermit's seclusion is a means of saving his soul from the damning influences of the world about him, Blasius' flight is motivated by the desire to preserve the most precious of individual possessions, the capacity to feel. Blasius, an echo of Werther, embodies the high valuation of "Fühlbarkeit" – Werther's term.

The theme of martyrdom, implicit in the treatments of Lenz's hermit and of Goethe's in *Satyros*, cannot be associated with Blasius (as it cannot with Simplicissimus), because his flight represents for him a personal salvation, a fulfillment of his deepest personal longing.

We have seen that the interpretation of nature, itself, as opposed to that of society, plays an unimportant role in Lenz's *Die Kleinen* and in Lessing's *Der Eremit*. In Klinger's *Sturm und Drang*, as in Goethe's *Satyros*, the hermit's relationship to nature counterbalances his reaction to society. In *Satyros*, Goethe's hermit is the protagonist of a procreative nature as the revelation of divine purpose, which can be grasped only through individual experiencing – nature and religion are, in a sense, one. In *Sturm und Drang*, a specifically religious aspect is lacking, but both Blasius and Goethe's hermit substitute the world of nature for that of a deficient society – in this respect, the attitudes of both figures toward life is positive; their rejection of society leads to the discovery of an eternal phase of life. For both Klinger's and Goethe's solitaries, nature is a living, breathing organic cosmos – although it is a more narrowly emotional force in nature which speaks to Blasius.

With the exception of Blasius, all of the hermit figures which we have analyzed are conceived in a traditionally Christian manner – they are holy men. The religious motif is strongly implicit in each of them (even though in Lessing's poem false religiosity is put to the lash). In the cases of all figures (but Lessing's) it is the reaction to society which specifically brings about the hermit's withdrawal. Only *Satyros* and *Sturm und Drang* point to the hermit's discovery of nature as a cosmos which contrasts with the shortcomings of social life.

In contrast to the others, Blasius will be a quite secular recluse; in this regard, he is untraditional, and represents a departure. Nature becomes for him the sinecure of the man who is misunderstood by society.

The view of nature in *Sturm und Drang* differs from that in *Satyros* in so far as Blasius finds in it not so much the revelation of an absolute divine purpose but, rather, the spring of eternal feeling. This is a conception which we find developed to great depth in the hermits of the romantic poets – in Lenau's *Marionetten*. To be reemphasized is the fact that it is night, specifically, in nature, which draws Blasius into its sphere – another theme which, with its myriad interpretations, becomes one of the principal ones in Romanticism.

(5) The revolt against decadence in society and particularly against the upper classes is a recurrent theme in "Storm and Stress" literature. This theme is developed through the hermit figure in Lenz's *Die Kleinen*, and it is suggested in the conflict of Blasius, who rescues himself from the superficiality of the social world and flees into the healing realm of nature. In Satyros, the hermit is the exponent of nature as "Gottes Stadt"; he who trammels it violates divine order.

Gottfried Bürger couples these two themes in his stormy ballad, *Der wilde Jäger*. In this poem, a decadent, unprincipled aristocrat lays waste nature, the symbol of divine order, and is consequently punished for his sin by divine justice. Through his violation of nature, the "Wild- und Rheingraf" also becomes guilty of oppressing the peasant class, which is seen by the poet as closely related to nature and dependent upon it for a productive livelihood. The hermit, "der fromme Kläusner" is ultimately associated with the divine spirit of nature, and intercedes in its behalf before God.

Of the thirty-six strophes in the poem, the first twenty concern the flagrant vandalism of the Count, the climactic strophes (the twenty-first through the twenty-fourth) introduce the hermit with his warning and the Count's rejection of it.

In order to appreciate fully the significance of the hermit's role and the conception of nature which he defends, it is of importance to analyze briefly Bürger's treatment of the Count and his blasphemous devastation of the peaceful countryside. In accordance with Bürger's low Saxon provenience and in keeping with balladesque tradition, the characters receive a legendary, "sagenhafte" treatment. Bürger's work is, indeed, the finest poetic treatment of a famous low Saxon legend, several versions of which are to be read in the *Deutsche Sagen* of the Brothers Grimm – Ludwig Bechstein's version (in his *Märchen und Sagen*) is a prose narration of Bürger's ballad. The introduction of Jakob Grimm's *Deutsche Mythologie* makes reference to Hans von Hackelberg, the "wild Huntsman", a Hannoverian country squire. Grimm associates him through the Gothic origin of his name with Germanic paganism and Wodan. The King of the gods was envisioned as a rider in the northwestern Germanic area. He was the first leader of a "wütendes Heer" which raged across the countryside and through the skies. Because he, too, was the last legendary representative of old folk belief, Widukind, the Saxon prince, was identified with Wodan. Following his defeat at the hands of Charlemagne, he led his warriors on a wild ride across the Westphalian heath. This is of significance for our interpretation of the "Kläusner", since the Rheingraf thus must be understood also as an embodiment of paganism in opposition to the Christian hermit. Of striking interest is the fact that God's spokesman, the recluse, here is associated with nature, as we have said, while the pagan element, generally at one with nature, here violates God's creation.

The tone of blasphemy implicit in the Count's devastation of nature is present in the second strophe. It is Sunday and the dome of the cathedral gleams in the early morning sun –

(1. 9 ff.) "Zum Hochamt rufte dumpf und klar
Der Glocken ernster Feierklang.
Fern tönten lieblich die Gesänge
Der andachtsvollen Christenmenge."

The first strophe, however, has already shown us that the Count does not belong to the reverent community of the common folk. He pays no heed to the peaceful tolling of the bell; indeed, it is probably inaudible to him, since he is wildly exhorting his company to horse, while his baying pack is turned loose upon the placid countryside. The pending judgment of the Count and the precarious predicament of his soul are suggested not only by the direction of the hunt – (1. 13) "Rischrasch quer übern Kreuzweg gings" (the crossroad was a traditional burial spot for suicides and highwaymen) – but also by his position between the two mysterious riders who suddenly appear on either side of him (a variation of the Dürer engraving, "Ritter, Tod, und Teufel", perhaps of Marlowe's two angels in *Doctor Faustus*) (1. 17 ff.) "Des Rechten Ross war silbersblinken, Ein Feuerfarbner trug den Linken."

In spite of the angelic rider's warning that the hunting horn sounds ill in tune to choir and churchbell, the Count scarcely needs the urging of the sinister horseman –

(1. 39 ff.) "Was Glockenklang? Was Chorgeplärr?
Die Jagdlust mag Euch bass erfreun!
Lasst mich, was fürstlich ist, Euch lehren
Und Euch von jenem nicht betören!"

In this exhortation of the evil genius, the poet also identifies the wanton destruction of the hunt with the aristocracy ("was fürstlich ist"), and this class thereby receives a character symbolic of evil and rapacity. In the very same manner all of the figures in the poem have typical and symbolic attributes rather than individual ones.

The goal of the wild Count's hunt is, in itself, of sacred quality as a creature of nature and the paths of destruction which the Count follows in pursuing it lead him to damnation. Two specific acts of vicious oppression lead up to, and bring about his judgment. When the stag seeks refuge in the grainfield of a poor plowman, the Count and his party plunge after it. Heedless of the peasant's pleading, the Count, his company and his pack sweep over the field, lashing the farmer with whips and trampling under hoof the stalks of grain – the sole means of livelihood for the peasant. The second event reaches the very zenith of viciousness. The stag mingles with a herd of cattle, of which the owners are poor widows and other destitute folk. When the herdsman, under whose care the animals graze, begs the Count to take pity, the bestial nobleman sicks his blood-crazed hounds at the innocent creatures. The herdsman and his charges are gashed and torn while the stag manages to escape –

(1. 125-126) "Tief birgt sich's in des Waldes Mitte,
In eines Klausners Gotteshütte."

The verses tell us that the forest receives the persecuted animal into its darkness and we may understand, at the same time, that nature is taking unto itself its own – the center of the forest is the heart of nature, nearest the protecting arm of God – into the very hut of the hermit.

The precise spot in which the stag seeks refuge is (certainly through divine purpose) the "Gotteshütte" of the hermit, who has here a symbolic value even stronger and more inclusive than that of the other figures in the ballad. We have, to be sure, discussed the details of the hunt in some detail; we have done so, however, only in order to grasp accurately the full significance of the hermit's climactic role.

The center of the mysterious "deutscher Wald", to which the stag flees, is the very heart of nature. Bürger's conception begins this tradition which flowers in Romanticism. Here is the point of most intimate contact between God and his ordered creation and it is here that the hermit has his "Gotteshütte". This location indicates very plainly the poet's conception of him; dwelling farthest from man and society in the most intimate relationship to the creator, the hermit is the interpreter of the almighty will and protector of nature's inviolability. In this capacity, the hermit confronts the "Wild – und Rheingraf", whose rapacious pursuit leads to the very threshold of the hut, where the stag has taken refuge.

(1. 134) "Entweihe Gottes Freistatt nicht!"

Thus, the hermitage becomes an asylum for all God's creatures who are persecuted; it is a form of church, which the Count violates to his undoing, and the hermit speaks for God in upholding the inviolability of this asylum. He speaks, too, for all creatures which suffer from the cruelty of the nobility.

The hermit denounces the sin which the Count commits –

(1. 135-138) "Zum Himmel ächzt die Kreatur
Und heischt von Gott dein Strafgericht.
Zum letzten Male lass dich warnen,
Sonst wird Verderben dich umgarnen!"

The Count, in turn, ignores the warning of the hermit, as well as that of his angelic genius, and follows the urging of the evil one. At once he is enveloped by deathly stillness – that of eternity. The hermit fulfills not only the role of nature's intercessor, but also that of its prophet. He denounces the painful wrong which the Count, as a vicious representative of his tyrannical class, inflicts upon God's creatures and His creation.

God hears the cry of his "Sturm und Drang" hermit-prophet. Through the eternal silence into which he has been plunged, the

Count hears the terrible judgment which the hermit has called down upon his head –

(1. 175-180)   "Fleuch, Unhold, fleuch, und werde jetzt,
Von nun an bis in Ewigkeit,
Von Höll und Teufel selbst gehetzt!
Zum Schreck der Fürsten jeder Zeit,
Die, um verruchter Lust zu fronen,
Nicht Schöpfer noch Geschöpf verschonen!"

Thus Bürger unites through the climactic figure of the "Klausner" two of the principal themes of "Sturm und Drang" literature – the inviolate quality of nature and the tyranny of the aristocracy. The aristocracy, embodied in the Count, is attacked for its vicious oppression of the lower classes. These classes, represented, in turn, by the herdsman and plowman, are conceived by the poet as close to nature. They are integral with God's order in nature, while the count violates that order for his own sport and to satisfy his rapacity. In his pursuit of the white deer (and the horrible consequences of the hunt for the peasants), the Count is guilty of a grievous sin against the spirit of nature.

Nature is interpreted again in *Der wilde Jäger* as a living organic cosmos, the pattern of divine order. As in Goethe's play, the hermit is the embodiment of its spirit. We have seen, however, that he assumes quite different proportions here. The figure of the hermit is made typical rather than individual; he has a symbolic value. His seclusion in the heart of the forest makes him the interpreter of God's purpose and the defender of His creatures. (When the deer seeks refuge in the hermit's hut, one is inclined to think of St. Francis, as well as of St. Jerome and his docile beasts in Dürer's engraving.) Bürger's hermit accordingly defends divine order by opposing the Count's profligate destruction; his position as intermediary between God and nature also lends him a kind of prophetic power to call down the vengeance of God upon the profaning nobleman. He champions the cause of the peasant class, indirectly, through his confrontation of the Count.

The Count (representing the ruthless aristocracy and pagan wantonness has ridden roughshod over the commoners (represented by plowman and herdsman), but when he seeks to defile God's inviolate order (represented by the hermit) he meets his doom. The hermit is of a different order from the plowman and herdsman; he stands for divine institutions, not human (How much higher he stands than e.g. the dubious figure in young Lessing's poem!)

The embodiment of prophetic power in the hermit figure is common also to the solitaries in *Oberon, Heinrich von Ofterdingen,* and *Hyperion* (all in Chapter IV), where, of course, the developments and conceptions of the prophetic power varies widely with the interpretation of the hermit figure. In each of these cases, howvver, it is essentially inherent in the hermit's relationship to nature. The strong identification of the hermit with the spirit of nature is present in the works just mentioned, as well as in the "Waldvater" of Kerner's *Die Heimatlosen* (Chapter IV). In Bürger's ballad, of course, he acts in this capacity in defense of nature against the "Wild- und Rheingraf", the archtype of criminally wastrel nobility.

(6) In Lessing's *Nathan der Weise*, the hermit is not involved in a conflict with specific classes of society, as are the various "Sturm und Drang" hermits; nor does a conception of nature, itself, with which the hermit is associated, figure in it as a way of life opposing the "Unnatur" of social shallowness (as in Klinger's play) or that of a bestial nobility (as in Bürger's ballad). Yet a very particular conception of nature (in the abstract) does actually form the ideal content of Lessing's "Ideendrama"; it is the concept of a "natural" (or "reasonable") humanity – a profoundly "natural" way of life which does not constrict human relationships by the limits of outer form or restrictions of dogmatic prejudices, but which does look beyond these artificialities for the essentially "natural" humanity binding men together in tolerant and understanding brotherhood.

In contrast to Nathan, the central figure, both Al-Hafi and the lay-brother turn from the world to preserve their ideals. In this respect, they serve as foils to Nathan who perseveres in an active life to the end that he may demonstrate to others a living experience of the pure humanity in which he believes. Al-Hafi's reaction to society is an absolute rejection of it, while the "Klosterbruder", a former hermit who had been driven from his abode by marauders, patiently performs the distasteful services required of him by the Patriarch only until such time as a new hermitage may be assigned to him.

Al-Hafi, the Dervish [1] is one of Lessing's most original and interesting characters, although he is only a minor one. Lessing's plan for a dramatic sequel to *Nathan, Der Derwisch (Theatralischer Nachlass, Lessing's Werke*, Bd. 10, p. 320) suggests that the poet may have regretted Al-Hafi's early departure for the wilderness at the end of the second act. The subject of this "Nachspiel" would have been Al-Hafi's return from hermithood into the world (see also the letter – *An Karl Lessing, den 15. Januar 1779 – Lessing's sämtliche Schriften, Briefe, Teil II*). Not only did this minor character strongly interest his own creator, but he also attracted the attention of Klinger, who composed a fantastic comedy, *Der Derwisch*, which appeared in 1780 (*F. M. Klinger, Dramatische Jugendwerke*, Bd. III).

[1] „Bettelmönch im Islam, ursprünglich individueller Asket" – *Schweizer Lexikon*.

The hero of Klinger's comedy, however, has little in common with Lessing's Moslem beyond his designation as Dervish in the title and a similar desire to flee to the Ganges, but with a lovely redbearded Fatime – (V, 1 – Beginning) "Süsse Seele, kümmere dich nicht, folg mir an Ganges, das Ende deiner und meiner Noth! Dort wird die Freude deines Lebens wiederkehren! Dort singt die Nachtigall in grünen Büschen, die Collibris hüpfen in deinen Schoos." (Klinger's hero does not function as a hermit at any stage of the dramatic action, and could not justifiably be included in this study.)

Al-Hafi, Lessing's Dervish, is motivated by an ideal of humanity as lofty as that which he recognizes in his friend, Nathan, but, unlike Nathan, he fears a situation which might involve a compromise of it. Rather than jeopardize his way of life and, therefore, himself in his own eyes, he withdraws from the world of everyday affairs.

When Lessing first introduces him (I, 3 – *Lessing's Werke*, Bd. 2 –), Al-Hafi has been tempted by his better self into a position which makes such a compromise inevitable for him. He appears in the splendid costume of Defterdar, the treasurer of Saladin, and astonishes his old friend, who cannot reconcile such magnificence with the character of the Dervish – for Al-Hafi has given up his individuality to become an official –

(1. 380)   "Ich dachte mir nur immer,
            Der Derwisch – so der rechte Derwisch – woll
            Aus sich nichts machen lassen."

The Dervish is supposed to live sufficient unto himself, apart from the world for the good of his soul; he depends for his subsistence upon the alms-giving public – this conception of the Moslem ascetic is, of course, strikingly similar to that of the traditional Christian hermit (as in the Introduction).

Al-Hafi accepted the position because he succumbed to a temptation to gratify his noble instincts. The temptation was the more insidious in that it struck him through his better self. This is what he confesses, essentially, in the lines which answer those of Nathan –

(1. 363 ff.)   "Dass ich kein rechter (Derwisch) bin,
               mag auch wohl wahr sein.
               Zwar wenn man muss –".

Nathan forces the issue to disclose the nature of his friend's problem and to ascertain whether Al-Hafi's garb corresponds to any change in the inner man –

(1. 384 ff.)   "Muss! Derwisch! – Derwisch muss?
               Kein Mensch muss müssen, und ein Derwisch müsste?
               Was müsst er denn?"

Nathan's question as to what a Dervish, or any man, "must" do evokes an answer typical of the steadfast nature of Al-Hafi. At the same time, the answer reveals that it is his deep humanity which has placed him in his new and inappropriate office –

(1. 386)   "Warum man ihn recht bittet,
                Und er für gut erkennt: das muss ein Derwisch."

Al-Hafi's dissatisfaction with his situation has its immediate roots in the character of the noble and over-generous Sultan. Saladin is determined to administer alms to all those in need (1. 408-410), with the result that his private coffers are depleted by sunset of each day in spite of the revenues which fill them in the morning. Al-Hafi's attitude is that of an idealistic absolutist; he is unwilling to distribute alms from a limited amount of funds, for he conceives it to be unjust and inhuman to deny those whose hands remain empty when the treasury is depleted. It is this attitude, essentially, which motivates his return to hermithood.

    The Dervish had let himself be seduced into his position as Defterdar, not by any desire to change his lot (1. 453-457), but by an invitation which flattered his better self. Saladin had become displeased with the coldness of the former treasurer – a man who had questioned each recipient of alms to determine the degree of his desserts. Therefore he chose the idealistic Dervish as his man, for only a beggar could know how to give graciously to another one –

(1. 473 ff.)   "Al-Hafi gleicht verstopften Röhren nicht,
                Die ihre klar und still empfangenen Wasser
                So unrein und so sprudelnd wiedergeben.
                Al-Hafi denkt; Al-Hafi fühlt wie ich!"

Al-Hafi had assumed the proffered office without having foreseen the threat to his idealistic well-being. In his conversation with Nathan, he is enraged and disgusted, first of all because he had permitted himself to be blinded by flattery –

(1. 458 ff.)   "Weit etwas abgeschmackters!
                Ich fühlte mich zum erstenmal geschmeichelt;
                Durch Saladins gutherz'gen Wahn geschmeichelt."

He seems to himself to be a fool's fool ("wie 'nes Gecken Geck!") in that he is attempting to execute Saladin's order to satisfy ever increasing needs with an ever decreasing treasury.

    There are two serious corollaries to this somewhat humorous predicament and both of them are threats to Al-Hafi's way of life – first –

(1. 484 ff.) "Es wär nicht Geckerei, des Höchsten Milde,
　　　　　　Die sonder Auswahl über Bös und Gute
　　　　　　Und Flur und Wüstenei, in Sonnenschein
　　　　　　Und Regen sich verbreitet, – nachzuaffen,
　　　　　　Und nicht des Höchsten immer volle Hand
　　　　　　Zu haben?"

The act of giving is a godly one; to dispense alms to the needy is to follow the example of the divine creator, who gives of himself unceasingly and without discrimination to all. To ape God's generosity without being able to satisfy all those in need is a blasphemy to Al-Hafi. The second ramification involves the self-deception in his assumption of the office of Defterdar –

(1. 491 ff.) "Was es wäre
　　　　　　Nicht Geckerei, an solchen Geckereien
　　　　　　Die gute Seite dennoch auszuspüren,
　　　　　　Um Anteil, dieser guten Seite wegen,
　　　　　　An dieser Geckerei zu nehmen? He?"

Here Al-Hafi reveals not only his power of self-analysis, but also his awareness of the psychological danger in which he has placed himself. He recognizes the generosity which motivates Saladin, but to share in it for the illusory satisfaction of his own ego constitutes a breach of his ideal. The cultivation of the purest humanity is not compatible with the materialistic problems of society – to give to all in need would be godly, to give only to some, unjust and blasphemous. Nathan voices his understanding of Al-Hafi's dilemma with dry humour when he suggests that his eccentric friend depart for his wilderness on the Ganges (1. 496), since, in the company of men, he may forget his own humanity.

Having learned that Nathan has been summoned to the Sultan (1. 1425-26), Al-Hafi considers himself responsible for the inevitable ruin of his friend both spiritually and materially (for it was through Al-Hafi that Sittah's attention was attracted to the wise and noble Jew – 1. 1034). Convinced that Nathan is destined to succeed him as Defterdar, and completely disillusioned by his own experience, Al-Hafi cannot bear to watch the decline and ruin of his friend (1. 1443 ff.).

Nathan, as we have indicated, contrasts sharply with Saladin in the mind of Al-Hafi – Nathan, who never lends that he may always have something to give, embodies ideal humanity, while Saladin's well-meant generosity is actually based on half-truth.

Even though his eccentric absolutism makes Al-Hafi the only humorous figure in the play, the kernel of his character consists in his unwillingness to compromise with his idealism –

(l. 1485 ff.)   "Ich, der ich nie für mich gebettelt habe,
                 Soll nun für andre borgen, Borgen ist
                 Viel besser nicht als betteln: so wie leihen,
                 Auf Wucher leihen, nicht viel besser ist
                 Als stehlen."

The essence of Al-Hafi's philosophy of life is that a truth, an ideal, cannot exist if it is compromised – a half-truth is no truth. As our analysis of his motives in becoming Defterdar and of his reaction to the office have disclosed, life in society would require dealing in half-truth. Distrusting the temptation to self-deception, which exists in society for the idealist, and, in addition, feeling responsible for the pending ruin of his friend, Nathan, Al-Hafi resolves to depart for the Ganges. The ideal man lives for his ideal and, for the Dervish, that is possible only in contemplative isolation –

(l. 1489)   "Unter meinen Ghebern, an
             Dem Ganges, brauch ich beides nicht
             (Borgen, Betteln) und brauche
             Das Werkzeug beider nicht zu sein."

In a final attempt to save his friend from ruin, Al-Hafi urges Nathan to become a hermit with him –

(l. 1492)   "Am Ganges nur gibts Menschen. Hier seid Ihr
             Der einzige, der noch so würdig wäre,
             Dass er am Ganges lebte."

In their common devotion to human ideals, Nathan and Al-Hafi are much alike; that is the basis of their friendship and of Nathan's admiration for the Dervish –

(l. 1515 ff.)   "Der wahre Bettler ist
                 Doch einzig und allein der wahre König.'"

They differ, essentially, in that the course of Nathan's relationship with the other characters of the play reveals in him an active and optimistic philosophy of life; this is also evident in his hesitation in following Al-Hafi to the Ganges. As the Dervish shrewdly observes, Nathan only hesitates because he is seeking reasons for not going. Al Hafi's departure, on the other hand, is based partially upon a negative reaction to the pressure of social (financial) expediency – as we have pointed out, he fears the temptation to which an idealist is susceptibe in society, that of self-deception, through the best of motives, which would compromise the ideal, itself.

There is criticism of the ideal of hermithood impliciti n Lessing's portrayal of Al-Hafi. He is admirable in his honesty, his hatred of delusion and pretense, and in his humanitarian impulses. His solution, however, has a negative, unfruitful aspect. He has not the strength, as Nathan implies (1. 496-499), to be human among men; he can love his fellow-men only when he is away from them. His only salvation is flight from the world. Yet, there is, as we have said, a positive aspect of Al-Hafi's return to hermithood. The lines (1489 ff.) quoted on the preceding page connote an intense sense of pride and integrity, which has its roots in a profoundly ethical approach to life. Al-Hafi revolts against being the instrument of borrowing and lending – such activity is unworthy of the highest humanity, and amounts to complete degradation of man and ideal. His withdrawal from society is, in this regard, the fullest expression possible of his refusal to compromise (we need not comment upon the extent to which this attitude is representative of Lessing's).

The second hermit figure in Lessing's drama, the "Klosterbruder", stands in strong contrast to his Moslem counterpart, Al-Hafi. Although he does not appear as a hermit in the course of the play, technically, we know that he has been one (1. 2935) and that he is only biding his time, until he may return to contemplative isolation (1. 2950). Since Al-Hafi's full realization of his problem was the product of rationalization and its origin was perhaps due to a lapse in his clear-sightedness, the impetuous Dervish quickly remedied the threat to his idealistic well-being by returning immediately to hermithood. The "Klosterbruder", however, is portrayed as a simpler man than the intellectual Moslem and, as a true and humble Christian (as opposed to the Patriarch), his humility and perseverance in carrying out tasks distasteful to him fit him well.

In the scene which first introduces the lay-brother (I, 5), we are given an accurate and complete picture of the disgraceful and degrading errands which the poor man is forced to undertake for the Patriarch.

It is interesting to note how Lessing lets both of these hermit figures make their initial appearances engaged in acitivities foreign and degrading to them as individuals. When we first see the lay-brother (I, 4), he has been ordered by the Patriarch to sound out the Templar for a plot against the life of his (and the Templar's) protector, Saladin (1. 660-678) – the obscure but true Christian, living for his peace in God and motivated by feelings of deepest humanity is made the tool of a personified travesty of both concepts. It is, of course, apparent in his repetition of, "meint der Patriarch" (1. 683, 684, 689, 695), that the lay-brother wishes to disown any personal connection with the project of his superior. He expresses his personal reaction only once during the discussion; it is when he learns that the Templar owes Saladin his life that he interjects a heart-felt "Pfui!" (1. 689) into his exposition of the Patriarch's plans.

Lessing's general techniques in presenting both Al-Hafi and the lay-brother are similar. Both have been hermits in the past, and during the play we see both occupied in activities ill-befitting their modes of life. The Dervish, however, was, as we have seen, faced with an idealistic-ethical problem of humanity, which he solved for himself by clear and rational self-analysis. The problem of the lay-brother also involves the problem of higher humanity but, in him, it is treated from the more specifically religious approach; there is, in him, something more of feeling, rather than of rationalism.

The lay-brother is an embodiment of simplicity, humility and dutifulness – a lay-brother took only the vow of obedience. His basic urge is to live away from human society, but so long as he must remain in it, he is gentle and submissive.

In the scene we have just briefly discussed, the lay-brother's very suppression of his own personal reaction to the scurrilous proposals would suggest an inner horror and disgust, an almost conscious attempt to free himself from any connection with the words he utters. It is much later in the course of the dramatization that the lay-brother appears again (IV, 1), and this scene (again with the Templar) bears directly upon the initial one (I, 4). In an opening monologue, the "Klosterbruder" gives definite expression to his feeling about the tasks assigned, and he also tells us, to some extent, why he had become a hermit.

From the first line (1. 2381 – "Ja, ja! er hat schon recht, der Patriarch!"), we may assume that he has been reprimanded by the vile potentate for his failure to obtain the Templar's services in the plot against Saladin. The simple and honorable "Klosterbruder" concedes that his superior is quite right, that he has had no success in carrying out this or other such tasks. He cannot understand why he should be burdened with such orders, for it is most contrary to his nature. He is not disposed by nature to thrust his nose everywhere, to have a hand in everything –

(1. 2385)   "(mag) Mein Näschen nicht in alles stecken; mag
             Mein Händchen nicht in allem haben."

The use of the diminutives quoted above very clearly conveys contempt for the extensive meddling of the priesthood in affairs which not only do not concern them, but which are scarcely worthy of any whose lives should be dedicated to God alone. Thus the lay-brother strikes a theme which is an overtone to the broader subject of the drama: true humanity is not the exclusive property of a particular confession, nor is religion in a deeply human sense the exclusive property of the clerus. On the contrary, the Patriarch and the monastic society busy themselves with affairs which have nothing whatever to do with true religion (or true humanity). Just as Al-Hafi embodied an uncompromising idealism which he found could be preserved only by leaving society, so the "Klosterbruder" finds, ironically enough, that his purpose in life runs counter to that of the monastic society which surrounds him –

(1. 2387 ff.) "(Bin) Ich darum aus der Welt geschieden, ich
Für mich; um mich für andre mit der Welt
Noch erst recht zu verwickeln?"

Like Al-Hafi, he has the hermit's instinct to keep himself free from sullying alliances with the world. For the "Klosterbruder" the life among "Pfaffen" is the very antithesis of a life dedicated to God; this his experience with the Patriarch has conclusively proved to him.

That this is his innermost conviction, the ensuing conversation with the Templar brings out most pointedly. The scene takes place in a corridor of the cloister, and, consequently, when the good brother catches sight of the Templar, he is both surprised and disappointed, for he is convinced that the knight has reconsidered the Patriarch's proposition. The expression which he lends to his disappointment portrays explicitly his reaction to the unsavory task which he had earlier performed and indirectly his words convey also his contempt for its source –

(1. 2395 ff.) "Der liebe Gott, der weiss,
Wie sauer mir der Antrag ward, den ich
Dem Herrn zu tun verbunden war. Er weiss,
Ob ich gewünscht, ein offnes Ohr bei Euch
Zu finden; weiss, wie sehr ich mich gefreut,
Im Innersten gefreut, dass Ihr so rund
Das alles, ohne viel Bedenken, von
Euch wies't, was einem Ritter nicht geziemt."

Indeed, the proposed assassination of Saladin would ill become the honor of any knight, particularly one who owes his life to the intended victim of the foully planned murder. How much less does its hellish planning befit a Patriarch, an authority over priests and the Christian community? The antipathy of the "Klosterbruder" toward the Patriarch and all he stands for is immanent in his wonder at the Templar's intent to ask advice of the potentate. His wonder mounts when he realizes that the Templar has not come to the cloister regarding the Patriarch's proposed plot, but concerning a matter which the knight describes as "ziemlich pfaffisch" –

(I. 2424 ff.) "Gleichwohl fragt der Pfaffe
Den Ritter nie, die Sache sei auch noch
So ritterlich."

"Der Pfaffe" represents for the lay-brother the least desirable or trustworthy source of serious counsel; the Patriarch is, to him, the absolute antithesis of the godly man. The Templar, however, distinguishes between the Christian in the Patriarch and the man's true nature; his problem concerns the Christian, not the officious potentate. Consequently, he turns to the lay-brother, who possesses the ingredient lacking in his superior ("Seid Ihr mein Patriarch!") – pure humanity, pure religion, is not a form which cloaks the individual, but is the man, himself. The "Klosterbruder", nevertheless, is quite unwilling to share the Templar's problem; he reveals in his reaction his instinctive aversion to entanglements with social responsibilities –

(1. 2448 ff.) "Nicht weiter, Herr, nicht weiter!
Wozu? – Der Herr verkennt mich. – Wer viel weiss,
Hat viel zu sorgen; und ich habe ja
Mich *einer* Sorge nur gelobt. –"

Lessing represents hermithood in both the Dervish and the "Klosterbruder" as involving a desire to shed human responsibilities; the weakness and flaw of the hermit-solution is that it is based upon flight from the world instead of struggle with it. He does not wish to know the nature of the Templar's query because it would, under the circumstances, preoccupy him to an extent beyond his capacity to cope with it. The sincere and virtuous "Klosterbruder" retires, in principle, to his former hermithood (cf. quotation above), to the life dedicated to God, alone; as we have seen, this life, or "Lebenseinstellung" of the lay-brother has nothing whatever to do with the ungodly, scurrilous meddling of the Patriarch – his problem cannot concern the man of sincerity and virtue. This attitude indicates the cloister-brother's attempt to maintain "spiritual hermithood" beside his opposite number, the Patriarch. He retreats, of course, not only from the Patriarch, but, as we have suggested, from the world with its responsibilities.

Thus we see that Lessing's "Klosterbruder" hermit represents not only a parallel in the spiritual realm to Al-Hafi, the Moslem exponent of humanity in the ethical-idealistic realm, but he also becomes the antithesis of the Patriarch. The juxtaposition of the Patriarch and the "Klosterbruder" is pointedly illustrated by two scenes – IV, 2 and IV, 7. In the first of these, we need refer only to the Patriarch's response when the Templar informs him that Recha, as a destitute foundling, would have perished, had Nathan not taken her into his house. In spite of the fact that the Jew has been a loving father to her, the Patriarch sees only Nathan's neglect in not having her baptized –

(1. 2456 ff.) "Tut nichts! der Jude wird verbrannt!
– Denn besser,
Es wäre hier im Elend umgekommen,
Als dass zu seinem ewigen Verderben
Es so gerettet ward."

Even the inhumanly officious sham religiosity of the Patriarch has no deep roots, for there is not substance enough, ironically, in his inhumanity to hold them. When he realizes that the Templar has Saladin's ear (1. 2583 ff.), the Patriarch gives up his decision to seek Saladin's aid in punishing Nathan (1, 2570 ff.) (whose identity the Templar rightfully withholds), for he fears the influence of the man to whom the Sultan had shown grace – it is likely, too, that he fears the Templar because the latter has knowledge of the vile plot against Saladin's life. Finally, the Patriarch passes off the entire question as a hypothetical problem –

(1. 2599 ff.) "(Das wär so wiederum ein Auftrag für
Den Bruder Bonafides.) – Hier, mein Sohn!"

This conclusion to the scene is filled with acid irony and also with deep truth, for, in the Patriarch's decision to pass the matter on to the lay-brother (aptly characterized by his name – cf. quote above) the problem falls, in reality, into the hands of the sincere, godly man who, for once, has a "task" worthy of him – a "task" which does not immediately concern the Patriarch as long as he fears to carry it out, himself, in his accustomed inhuman manner.

The second of the scenes to which we have referred (IV, 7) contrasts the "Klosterbruder" definitively with his superior; it also completes Lessing's portrait of the lay-brother's character in relation to his hermithood. In the scene discussed above, the poet had delineated the Patriarch mercilessly as an example of the clerus whose "religion" has nothing to do with humanity or God. In the present scene (IV, 7), the lay-brother's analysis of the problem regarding Recha's upbringing reveals his "natural", or pure, humanity, his compassion which transcends outer forms –

(1. 3017 ff.) "Wenn nur das Mädchen sonst gesund und fromm
Vor Euern Augen aufgewachsen ist,
So blieb's vor Gottes Augen, was es war."

Had Nathan given the child over to be brought up as a Christian by others, it would not have received the love which was its due and which Nathan was able to give the daughter of his friend. The profound understanding of the "Klosterbruder" prompts Nathan to tell of the ghastly deaths of his wife and seven sons (3039-45) and of his gratitude to God, who gave him Recha to supplant, in part, his tragic loss (1. 3063-66). The painful but heart-warming tale inspires the good brother to the exclamation which, perhaps, best sums up his compassion and humanity –

(1. 3067 ff.) "– Bei Gott, Ihr seid ein Christ.!
　　　　　Ein bessrer Christ war nie!"

The "Klosterbruder" means here the pervading spirit of any religion worthy of man – love – rather than of any superficially distinguishing quality. He is, as we have seen, a man who feels spiritually and universally. He calls Nathan a "Christian", because his own religion conveys to him spiritual strength. (He can think of no higher praise, nevertheless, of Nathan's pure humanity than to call him a true Christian; in his simple mind, he associates such feeling as Nathan's with that which he considers characteristic of his own religion – there is, therefore, a sectarian coloring in the lay-brother's expression of human understanding.)

This scene also provides the most specific information about the cloister-brother's hermithood. There are elements in his background which remind us involuntarily of certain motifs in *Simplicissimus*. The "Klosterbruder" had been a trooper in the service of Recha's father, Wolf von Filnek, a Crusader, eighteen years earlier (1. 2970-2981). When his wife died shortly after the child's birth, the crusader sent the trooper with Recha to his friend, Nathan; the latter was to care for the child, until the father returned from battle. Wolf von Filnek, however, fell at Askalon (1. 2986) and the trooper preserved the "Brevier" which eventually provides information regarding the interrelationship of the major characters. We do not know specifically why the trooper became a hermit, but we may assume that (like Simplicius' father) he was horrified at the pillage and destruction of war, and, therefore, sought peace and salvation in a life of lonely contemplation. It is also possible that sorrow over the death of Wolf von Filnek (1. 2983 ff.) was an additional motive.

The cause of interruption in the lay-brother's hermithood was beyond his control. He had been taken from his cell near Jericho by Arab marauders who destroyed it (1. 2935 ff.). Having escaped from them, he fled to the Patriarch to obtain from him another hermitage where he might spend the rest of his days in God's service

(1. 2942 ff.) "Allwo ich meinem Gott in Einsamkeit
　　　　　　　Bis an mein selig Ende dienen könne."

(It is interesting to note that the lay-brother's first mountain hermitage, Quarantana, was the alleged scene of Christ's temptation, where He fasted forty days (hence its name); it was frequently the abode of medieval hermits – see *Anmerkungen, V. 2936, Lessings Werke*, p. 76). As we have seen, the "Klosterbruder" has suffered during his stay in the cloister because of the incompatibility of his adopted way of life with that of the nefarious Patriarch; yet he has remained true to himself. In contrast to the Patriarch, Lessing chose to represent in the "Klosterbruder" a deeply human and compassionate Christianity. To do so, he created in the lay-brother a sincere and simple man (who cannot even read – 1. 3108) – a man of the lower classes ("ein Reitknecht") who is motivated by natural feeling and devotion to God. In this respect, he contrasts also with the more intellectual Al-Hafi (a chess enthusiast) who might be designated as an idealistic and ethical rationalist (that is not to say that he is not also devoted to God, for we have seen the interpretation of blasphemy which he applied to his particular situation).

If the "Klosterbruder" was influenced initially in becoming a hermit by his war experience and his devotion to God, he has, since, evolved further reasons for wishing to return to hermithood –

(1. 2950 ff.) "Da bin ich itzt, Herr Nathan; und verlange
Des Tags wohl hundertmal auf Tabor. Denn
Der Patriarch braucht mich zu allerlei,
Wovor ich grossen Ekel habe."

(Tabor is the mount of transfiguration – cf. reference to *Anmerkungen*, p. 76, quoted above.)

The return to isolation will mean for the "Klosterbruder", in addition to his original longing for peace in God, a flight from the official representatives of a dogmatic and officious way of life which impedes and degrades the man of genuine devotion and virtue. While Al-Hafi, the idealist, flies from a society of false and (to him) blasphemous magnanimity, the "Klosterbruder" will depart from a society of sham religiosity and downright wickedness. It is not, however, only from the Patriarch and such men that he flees, but from all human society; he wishes to have no part of the world, for it is an impediment to complete devotion to God. We may add, nevertheless, that, of all the hermit figures in this study (with the possible exception of Trevrizent in the Introduction) who are conceived in a traditionally Christian manner, the "Klosterbruder" represents the deepest and most moving expression of Christianity, itself. But, in the portrayal of both Al-Hafi and the "Klosterbruder", Lessing does also imply a criticism of the negative and socially unfruitful solution of religious problems by hermithood.

(7) While in Lessing's drama both Al-Hafi and the "Klosterbruder" wish to dwell apart from society to preserve a conviction which is, to them, a way of life, Chamisso's romantic hermit, Peter Schlemihl, flees from society because of the loss of something which belongs intrinsically to him as a social individual – his shadow. Schlemihl's relationship to society is based upon this particular

object (or, rather, his lack of it). In this respect, the meaning of the shadow is of great importance; Oskar Walzel, in his introduction to *Chamissos Werke* (Deutsche-National-Literatur, p. LVII-LVIII), lists an overwhelming number of interpretations of the shadow's symbolic meaning. To attribute to the shadow a specific value or significance, however, runs counter to the theme of this "Märchen". Thomas Mann refers to the shadow in his essay, *Chamisso* (*Essays of Three Decades*, p. 257), where he calls it "a symbol of all bourgeois solidity and human belongingness"; Walzel treats of it as a kind of "Scheinwert" (p. LX – cf. reference to Walzel above). To endow the shadow with more definite characteristics than the writers just cited have done would rob the Schlemihl-hermit theme of its universality; it is precisely the indefiniteness of the shadow as a concept which lends to Chamisso's tale much of its depth. Chamisso, himself, supported this stand in the preface to the French edition of 1838 (*Chamissos Werke*, Bd. 2, p. 285 and p. 458), in which he answered with elegant sarcasm the queries of those who desired to know for their learned edification, the explicit meaning of the shadow (of course his explanation explained nothing). With tasteful humor, he cited a scientific definition of the shadow from a treatise on elementary physics, and summed up by indicating the theme of the tale – "Die Finanzwissenschaft belehrt uns hinlänglich über die Wichtigkeit des Geldes; die des Schattens ist minder allgemein anerkannt. Mein unbesonnener Freund hat sich nach dem Gelde gelüsten lassen, dessen Wert er kannte, und nicht an das Solide gedacht" ("Das Solide" is the French "le solide" referring in the treatise to the shadow – Chamisso plays on the double meaning of this word in the original French).

The shadow is, then, an intrinsic possession or characteristic of the individual as a member of society. It has no value as long as one has it; its lack, however, is of alarming importance, for the absence of the shadow sets Schlemihl apart from society – without it he does not "belong". Having incurred a kind of "faustian" guilt through the exchange of his shadow for the magic purse of Fortunatus, Schlemihl renounces all ties with society, including his wealth. His hermithood is his salvation, for in it he turns to nature, and lives for his better self – Schlemihl's hermithood becomes the apotheosis of individualism which achieves independence of society and its "Scheinwerte" through painful experience.

The tale takes the form of a memoir written by Schlemihl from his hermitage, which he has allegedly delivered to his friend, Chamisso, in Berlin (during the latter's absence – Chamisso was at Kunersdorf composing the tale). This form permits the hermit to look back upon his experiences, and evaluate them as developments toward his final way of life – as in *Hyperion* or *Die Braut von Messina*

(1. 2104 – "Von dem Berg der aufgewälzten Jahre"), as well as in Eichendorff's *Eine Meerfahrt* (Don Diego's rocky island in the south seas). Such hermits, forever removed from the world, survey their arduous progress through it.

The instigation to acquire the wealth which costs him his shadow is occasioned when the modest and unprepossessing Schlemihl arrives at the garden party of wealthy Herr John (Chap. I, *Chamissos Werke*, Bd. 2). He is received very well by his host (Schlemihl says with sarcasm) – "wie ein Reicher einen armen Teufel" (p. 292). During the initial conversation, John is scarcely aware of his poor visitor, and continues the apostrophe to wealth which is the subject of discourse among the assembled guests – "Wer nicht Herr ist wenigstens einer Million, der ist, man verzeihe mir das Wort, ein Schuft!" These words, of course, arouse the envy of Schlemihl, who views with wonder the effete doings of his host and party. The poor fellow's feeling of inferiority and longing is aroused; his exclamatory reaction to John – "O wie wahr!" – discloses the susceptibility which makes of him an easy mark for the subsequent bargaining of the "gray man". The effeteness of the society which treasures wealth so highly must be born in mind, as well as the fact that John has sold, not his shadow, but his soul to the gray man (Chap. VIII, p. 337), for Schlemihl's hermithood embodies a rejection of this society's standard of values, and thus it becomes the means of his salvation.

It is only when his "Schattenlosigkeit" becomes the butt of mockery, horror, and pity of all ages and sexes after his departure from John's estate that the first impact of Schlemihl's error strikes him. He hurls his gold into the streets to stave off attention, and climbs into a coach to weep over the lot which has befallen him – (II, p. 298) "Es musste schon die Ahnung in mir aufsteigen: dass, um so viel das Gold auf Erden Verdienst und Tugend überwiegt, um so viel der Schatten höher als selbst das Gold geschätzt werde –" – in other words, the world's perverse valuation of "Scheingüter" above true values. Schlemihl locks himself in his rooms, and hurls himself upon his heap of gold, wallowing in it in a fit of sensuous madness.

The more he seeks to rise in esteem, however, the more defiantly his lack of a shadow impedes Schlemihl's striving to attain happiness. At one of his soirees (III, end), the lovely Fanny, who had originally ignored him at John's, is attracted to him obviously because of his wealth (although she does not remember having met him before). The supercilious persiflage which Schlemihl has learned to use as commensurate with his social position impresses her greatly. Yet when she sees only her own shadow before her in the full moonlight, she falls into a swoon in spite of his wealth and effete polish. The incident bears out conclusively Schlemihl's anticipatory estimation of his lot as quoted previously – wealth may be of more importance to many than true virtue, but to all the "Scheinwert" which qualifies "belonging" is primary.

It is the unhappy experience with Mina, nevertheless, which brings Schlemihl's sense of guilt to its zenith; the outcome of the affair makes it possible for him to reject finally the pact which might have given him both wealth and shadow (as in the case of Herr John) – but at the price of his soul. This experience ripens to the extent that he is able eventually, also, to reject society and its standards for the hermithood in nature. The weight of the episode lies in the fact that Mina loves Schlemihl in spite of his wealth and in spite of his "Schattenlosigkeit." This she expresses (IV, p. 314) when her lover somewhat cryptically explains that his destiny is to be decided on the last day of the coming month (the day on which the gray man had promised to arrange a new bargain – II, end) – "ich habe keinen Anspruch an dich. – Bist du elend, binde mich an dein Elend, dass ich es dir tragen helfe." Her love for him remains constant even when she discovers that his shadow is missing (IV, end). On the evening following Schlemihl's declaration to Mina's father of his intent to marry her, he visits Mina in her garden. As he approaches her, she makes an involuntary motion (probably one of surprise or shock), and Schlemihl thinks at once of the evening with Fanny when he had exposed himself to the moonlight – but Mina "warf sich stille weinend an meine Brust. Ich ging." We may be assured that Mina had also observed the nature of his plight, but her father prefers to give his daughter's hand to Rascal – overriding his wife's suspicions, for that scoundrel is not only wealthy, but is in possession of a flawless shadow.

Although the gray man makes Schlemihl witness the family scene which breaks Mina's heart, the drive to rebel against "Scheinwert" remains dominant in him. He had previously refused to sign the contract which would have regained the shadow at the price of his soul (V, p. 320). So now, too, the "dunkler Drang" to save his soul even at the price of Mina's happiness manifests itself (VI, end -VII, p. 329) – when the gray man, holding parchment and pen, draws a drop of blood, Schlemihl is saved by a fainting spell. The faint, which Schlemihl characterizes as an event ("Ereignis") rather than a deed ("Tat"), is probably a result of the struggle in his heart between the desire to save Mina and the revulsion against any further dealing with the gray man. He respects, nevertheless, the necessity which drives his destiny and that of others like cogwheels in the great machine of life.

The burden of the entire experience with Mina has, as we have stated, the greatest importance as motivation for Schlemihl's turn inward to himself, for his development toward hermithood. His refusal to sign away his soul in order to regain his shadow adds Mina's heartbreak to his original guilt and, when he revives from his faint (VII, p. 330), she has been married to Rascal. Consequently the strongest existing motive for recovering the shadow is removed, and Schlemihl leaves the scene of his greatest guilt and deepest sadness, utterly alone – (VII, end) "und entfernte mich unter dem Mantel der Nacht von dem Grabe meines Lebens, unbekümmert, welchen Weg mein Pferd mich führen werde; denn ich hatte weiter auf Erden kein Ziel, keinen Wunsch, keine Hoffnung."

The loss of Mina throws Schlemihl completely upon himself and he accepts his lot as a man apart; this conscious acceptance of his fate renders possible, consequently, the decision which severs all ties forever with the gray man and with society, and leaves open the path to hermithood. In this state of mind, then, he is followed by the gray man (VIII) who, as he says, holds him fast by his shadow. When the odious gray gentleman concisely explains that a wealthy man must possess a shadow in the world, Schlemihl remains resolute – (VIII, p. 335) "Nachdem ich meine Liebe hingeopfert, nachdem mir das Leben verblasst war, wollt ich meine Seele nicht, sei es um alle Schatten der Welt, dieser Kreatur verschreiben." The shadow, the "Scheinwert" requisite to wealth and social standing, which had seemed earlier of such crucial importance, now, since the disheartening Mina "Erlebnis", becomes almost nothing when it is weighed against the soul – the individual, himself.

Thus it is clear to Schlemihl, as the gray man displays John's pale and distorted form to him on a lonely mountain gorge, that his wealth, the "Glücksäckel", binds him to his insidious companion. Wealth and shadow are inextricably connected with one another at the price of the soul. The condemnation which John's soul utters through its corpse-like lips crushes Schlemihl with its horrifying revelation, and he flings the magic purse into the abyss, freeing himself from the gray man and from wealth and shadow values henceforth.

Freed from the ghastly weight which had haunted him, Schlemihl lies down to rest. A lovely dream visits him, in which those he has loved best appear – Mina, Bendel (and Chamisso, himself) weaving graceful dance patterns over a lovely landscape – and all are without shadows (one is immediately reminded, of course, of "Anmutige Gegend", *Faust II*). To be sure, upon awakening Schlemihl remains an outcast because he has no shadow, but this state leads him to seek work in a mine, where his "Schattenlosigkeit" would be less obvious. Rainy weather ruins his shoes on the way and he acquires by accident the Seven-League Boots which reveal to him the wonders of nature on his round-the-world jaunt. This incident provides the final turning point in his career – (X, beginning) "Ich fiel in stummer

Andacht auf meine Knie und vergoss Tränen des Dankes – denn klar stand plötzlich meine Zukunft vor meiner Seele." Separated from society through "frühe Schuld", he turns to the realm of nature, the world of the man who lives for his better self. The love of the individualist for nature is not a sudden development in him, for it is inherent in the man who frees himself from social "Scheinwerte" – (X, beginning) "und meine Selbstzufriedenheit hat von dem Zusammenfallen des Dargestellten mit dem Urbild abgehangen". When Schlemihl passes through the Egyptian desert, and sees Thebes of the hundred gates, the obvious decision is made. (Thebes, the capital of upper Egypt, became in the fifth century A. D. the original site of Christian hermitages, and was the scene of many early martydoms – *Schweizer Lexikon*). Thus, Schlemihl goes not to the "Wald", as do most of the hermits in German literary tradition, but to the desert dwellings of the first Christian hermits (hermit, "Eremit" – from Greek "ἐρημίτησ", a "lone-dweller" – "ἐρήμοσ", lonely – cf. Merriam-Webster). He reverts to the most ancient Christian hermit tradition. Here Schlemihl decides to become a hermit, and selects the cave of a former solitary. He will spend his life as a recluse far from society, living for his better self and devoted to the study of nature and the natural sciences so dear to him (an interesting reflection of Chamisso's own botanic studies). The stay in the "Schlemihlium" affords him the opportunity to learn that Mina and Bendel, resigned to their early experience, have found happiness in charitable work. Schlemihl, however, has found himself, and adheres firmly to his newly discovered way of life – "willst du unter den Menschen leben, so lerne verehren zuvorderst den Schatten, sodann das Geld. Willst du nur dir und deinem bessern Selbst leben, o, so brauchst du keinen Rat."

For social "success," "Scheinwerte" such as shadows and gold are essential, but for the true individualist (the hermit) they are nothing.

Thus the hermit, Peter Schlemihl, embodies the extreme and concentrated individualism which casts off the questionable standards required by society. As the result of his Faustian struggle, he turns inward, and discovers solace in nature as a source of knowledge of the true world – the only world for the better self.

It is not surprising that, in the works previously discussed, those hermit figures who most strongly oppose the valid world of nature to the false standards of society belong to the "Sturm und Drang" –the analysis of the motivation for hermithood in *Satyros* and *Sturm und Drang* reveals this juxtaposition of values in the hermit (or "hermit-to-be", in the case of Blasius). In the cases of all hermit figures in this chapter, however, the conflicts involve a rejection of accepted social standards which are felt to be damaging to the integrity of the individual, or, at least, to his well-being. It is also not surprising that the majority of hermit figures in this chapter occur in "Storm and Stress" works, for that movement accentuated the positive and natural qualities of the individual in relationship to society (that this is also true of Lessing is understood – although, as we have seen, on a different plane).

It is interesting to note that, while the majority of the hermits discussed so far has been localized in the "Wald" (in pursuance of German love for the forest both in a religious and in a nature-sense), Schlemihl withdraws to the original locale of the earliest Christian hermits or "Wüstenväter" in the Thebaid.

Schlemihl's hermit solution is somewhat similar to Hyperion's. Both figures withdraw from society to timeless nature. In both works there is severe criticism of society: the hero saves his soul and finds contentment only by renouncing society for nature, the source of healing and innocence.

Chamisso's Schlemihl-hermit is a most opportune figure with which to conclude this chapter, for, just as Romanticism developed many of the themes of "Sturm und Drang", so Peter Schlemihl's development to hermithood embodies in its motifs most of the themes observed in the preceding hermit figures, together with the strong individualism typical of Romanticism (and of "Sturm und Drang").

Peter Schlemihl, nevertheless, also appears fittingly at the conclusion of this chapter because of the characteristics which make it transitional to the next. As our analysis of the motives for his hermithood have disclosed, the hermit, Schlemihl, reveals to an intenser degree the subjective state of mind in the struggle of the individual to retain his essential individuality in relationship to society – thus, too, he is similar to Klinger's Blasius in *Sturm und Drang*. In this respect, the theme of the tragic or unhappy love experience plays an important role. We have examined here the hermit in his relationship to society and his rejection of its values; in the next we see the essential personality of the hermit revealed by problems of a more intimate, subjective nature.

CHAPTER III

THE INNER CONFLICT

A. (1) In the two principal versions of Goethe's *Erwin und Elmire*, 1775 and 1787, Erwin retires to mountain peace, because his sincere and open expressions of love have not been returned, but even scorned by the coquettish Elmire. The atmosphere of the little operetta is light and full of rococo flavor. Although the work was frankly designed to delight, rather than to stir deeply, the arias allotted to both Erwin and Elmire are, as might be expected from Goethe, intense lyrical expressions of their emotions – this is also not surprising when one imagines in the verses echoes of the Goethe – Lili relationship.

The hermit theme differs slightly in the earlier version from that of the later one. In the variant of 1775, there is only Erwin, while that of 1787 contains two hermits – the deceased recluse, whose hermitage Erwin assumes, and Erwin, himself. The treatments of Erwin as a hermit vary also in several respects.

In the first version (*Der junge Goethe*, Bd. V), when we see Erwin working in the garden before his hut, it is apparent that his solitude has brought him anything but peace (p. 53). He has fled the world, as we know, because Elmire, who actually does love him, has seemed to mock his feeling (p. 47 ff.). Erwin's hermithood has not only brought no comfort, but it has aggravated his pain and sorrow; isolation has not created in him a resignation to his lot, but rather an emotional conflict which had not existed before – (p. 53) "Welchen Entschluss hab ich gefasst! Was hab ich gethan! Sie nicht mehr sehn! Abgerissen von ihr! Und fühlst du nicht, Armseliger, dass der beste Theil deines Lebens zurückgeblieben ist, und das übrige nach und nach traurig absterben wird!" Added to the sorrow over Elmire's treatment of him is the feeling that his resolution robs him of the doubtful satisfaction of ever seeing her again. Thus, Erwin's solitude occasions a state of mental torture. His flight hardly prevents him from seeing her lovely form before his mind's eye, while it does incite him to maddening curiosity as to whether she may be concerned at all about his fate. Although Erwin has become a hermit to still the pain of his heartbreak, he is aroused to longing for the life he has left. The latter aspect of his dualistic emotional condition conflicts, of course, with his firm decision to part from the world – (p. 54) "und mich umgibt die ewig einfache, die ewig neue Qual, dumpfer und peinigender, als die mich in ihrer Gegenwart fasste." The exposition of Erwin's emotions, his confused feelings, which are typical of the "Sturm und Drang" Goethe, finds its most intense expression in the aria which concludes Erwin's monologue –

(p. 54)
"Inneres Wühlen
Ewig zu fühlen;
Immer verlangen,
Nimmer erlangen;
Fliehen und streben,
Sterben und leben,
Höllische Qual
Endig einmal."

The restlessly tossing rhythms of this poem, anticipating the equally contradictory feelings of Klärchen's song, "Himmelhoch jauchzend/ Zum Tode betrübt", (absent from the 1787 version) convey through the pairs of contrasted verbs ending each of the first six verses ("Wühlen-fühlen," etc.) the hermit's inner struggle to attain peace of mind – the last two verses sum up the fervent wish which so far remains unfulfilled.

In this emotional state, therefore, Erwin finds the visit of Bernardo most unwelcome – Bernardo has also directed the repentant Elmire to the hermit that he may comfort her (thus he accomplishes the reconciliation of the lovers, p. 50-52). Bernardo is an intruder from the world which Erwin strives, with so little success, to thrust from his mind; his coming means increased renewal of the pangs which tear the hermit, and withhold from him the soothing calm of solitude. Consequently, Erwin presents a defiant attitude to Bernardo's entreaties to return. His unhappy experience has discolored all communal life in his eyes; perhaps this outlook is a subconscious means of maintaining his hermithood – (p. 55) "Der Welt? wie lieb ist mirs, dass ich mich heraus gerettet habe. Es hat mich gekostet; nun bin ich geborgen. Mein Schmerz ist Labsal gegen das, was ich in dem verfluchten Neste von allen Seiten auszustehen hatte." (Erwin refers indirectly, perhaps to his lack of means – cf. Erwin, p. 55 mid., and Olimpia, p. 44 bot.)

Erwin's hermithood represents a state in which he intends to retain himself by force of will – (p. 55) "Ich habe geschworen, ich kehre nicht zurück!" This is the case, because his solitary mountain abode has become a battleground of emotional drives, rather than a solace to the disappointment which brought him there. As a result, when Erwin unmasks himself to Elmire and the two rejoicing lovers return to a happy and harmonious life, the former hermit almost neglects taking leave of the hermitage which has been the scene of lonely suffering – (p. 65) "Ich gehe, und schaue mich nicht nach dir um! danke dir nicht! ehre dich nicht! sage dir kein Lebewohl, du freundlichste Wirthin meines Elends –." Yet he reproaches himself for this neglect (which is due to Elmire's charms – "Mädchen was macht Ihr uns nicht vergessen!"), and dedicates a tear to the hospitable little hut.

In this version of *Erwin und Elmire*, the recluse who seeks consolation in solitude because of disappointment in love is conceived as a sufferer, a victim, even when isolated, of an intense emotional dualism – the peace he struggles to attain is denied him. The older, wiser Bernardo, on the other hand, raises his voice (duet with Erwin, p. 55) against hermithood as being a solution for the weak, an expression of "Lebensunfähigkeit"; he praises the life of the citizen who earns his living, and creates a household –

> "Erdennoth ist keine Noth,
> Als dem Feig und Matten.
> Arbeit schafft dir täglich Brod.
> Dach und Fach und Schatten.
> Rings, wo Gottes Sonne scheint,
> Findst ein Mädchen, findst einen Freund,
> Lass uns immer bleiben!"

The hermit theme assumes somewhat different coloring in the operetta of 1787. (The material of both forms is traceable to Rousseau's *Devin du village* and a ballad in the *Vicar of Wakefield* – cf. *Der junge Goethe*, VI, p. 452 ff.). The "Sturm und Drang" character of the earlier form, which is apparent in Erwin's more violent emotional conflict, and to which the prose of the spoken passages strongly contributes, fades in the later work in favor of a rococo-elegiac tone. This is largely due, not only to the new verse setting and the supplanting of Olimpia and Bernardo by the additional pair of lovers, Rosa and Valerio, but, for our purposes, most particularly to the motif of the old, deceased hermit (and, obviously, to the transformation in Goethe, himself, between '75 and '87).

Where, in the form previously discussed, Erwin's hermithood occasions a consuming emotional conflict, the introduction of the old hermit, the former inhabitant of Erwin's chosen abode, changes the "Stimmung" to one of nostalgic or plaintive calm in the final version. Although the old hermit has already died before the action takes place, his influence in it is strong and we are given an accurate impression of him as a recluse.

It is Valerio who characterizes the recluse when he directs Elmire to him for comfort and consolation (unlike Bernardo, Valerio has no idea of Erwin's whereabouts). Even in Valerio's description of the path to the hermitage, a healing power is ascribed to the peaceful natural surroundings

(1. 284 ff.) "– es wird dir wohl
Auf diesem Wege werden, wohler noch,
Wenn du das Heiligtum erreichst."

The hermit draws spiritual strength from nature, which gives him the power to impart the calm of his spirit to others; thus, identified with the healing, eternal aspect of nature, the solitary is conceived as knowing more of life than others (cf. *Braut von Messina*, Part IV) – he possesses its inexpressible secrets –

(1. 291 ff.) "Und trügt mich nicht, was ich an ihm bemerkt,
Sein ungetrübtes freies Auge schaut
Die Ferne klar, die uns im Nebel liegt.
Die Melodie des Schicksals, die um uns
In tausend Kreisen klingend sich bewegt,
Vernimmt sein Ohr; und wir erhaschen kaum
Nur abgebrochene Töne hier und da."

Erwin is revealed (Zweiter Aufzug) singing his aria, "Ihr verblühet, süsse Rosen" (as in the early version), but its elegiac tone does not change in the monologue which follows it, but, rather, a veil of tranquil melancholy is spread over the unhappy love experience – a transparent veil, however, which lets Erwin's pain and sorrow be expressed in softer rhythms of poignant reflection. This pain, nevertheless, which is renewed through memory of Elmire's beauty, never assumes the violent proportions of the emotional conflict in the version previously discussed. Even though memory of Elmire increases his sorrow and longing in solitude, the reflective tone in Erwin's expression of it implies that he has found, at least, a measure of peace –

(1. 480 ff.) "Je tiefer sich die Sonne hinter Wolken
Und Nebel bergen mag, je trüber sich
Der Schmerz um meine Seele legt –"

and when his longing approaches in its intensity a desire to regain her fleeting image by returning to her (1. 495 ff.), he invokes the spirit of the ancient hermit, for the soothing tranquility of his soul still pervades the garden where he lies buried. (Erwin had received comfort from the harmonious man in times past, and, therefore, has chosen his dwelling-place for his own retreat.) When he thinks of his old mentor's example, peace comes over him and the phantom voice of Elmire is silent in his mind –

(l. 514 ff.)　"Welch ein Lispeln, welch ein Schauer
　　　　　　　Weht vom Grabe des Geliebten!
　　　　　　　Ja, es wehet dem Betrübten
　　　　　　　Sanften Frieden in das Herz."

Valerio, also, has resolved to seek seclusion, having lost patience with Rosa because of her petty jealousies –

(l. 377 ff.)　"Nein! Nein, ich folge jenem Trieb, der mir
　　　　　　　Schon lang den Weg zur Flucht gezeigt, schon lange
　　　　　　　Mich deiner Tyrannei auf ewig zu
　　　　　　　Entziehen hiess."

He, too, hopes to find the calm which solitude in nature has granted the old hermit (l. 529 ff.), and, dedicating his life to loneliness, he swears an oath to lofty forest and waterfall. Since Erwin is heir, in a sense, to the spiritual calm with which his predecessor had imbued the hermitage, Valerio's arrival is welcome to him (l. 551 ff.) – although, as in the prose version, his visitor occasions the return of visions from which he had found a measure of release (l. 582 ff.).

When the two girls appear and Elmire (l. 779 ff.) expresses her penitence, Erwin plays the role of comforting father-confessor, disguised in a robe (a new one in which the modest old hermit disdained to be buried) and in a beard improvised from Valerio's shorn blond locks.

After the joyous reconciliation has taken place, there is a note of thankfulness in the rejoicing of the lovers as they depart, for the hermitage of the kindly old recluse has brought harmony into their hearts. Even though Erwin admits –

(l. 885 ff.)　"Ohne Träne kann ich lassen
　　　　　　　Diese Hütte, dieses Grab" –

he feels no antipathy toward the retreat (as in the early version) but, rather, gratitude, for it gave him peace in time of his greatest need, and the spirit of the old hermit, which dominates the lonely hermitage, has, as it were, also given the lovers comfort and reunion –

(l. 887 ff.)　"Oft, durch unser ganzes Leben
　　　　　　　Bringen wir der stillen Hütte
　　　　　　　Neuen Dank und neue Bitte,
　　　　　　　Dass uns bleibe, was sie gab."

In this version of the "Singspiel," then, Erwin does find in hermithood a large measure of peace and consolation for his heartbreak, and the source of tranquility and comfort is nature. Most important in this connection, however, is the role which the old hermit plays, for, in spite of the fact that he is characterized only through the other persons, it is he whose spirit lends its calm to the hermitage. Thus, he embodies a kind of ideal of the hermit; identified with nature from which he has drawn a higher knowledge of life, he is able to impart to others the harmonious repose which he has found – that his influence may be felt even after his death testifies to the eternal harmony with nature in which he had lived. The interpretation of eternal calm in nature found embodied in this hermit figure is typical of Goethe; together with the longing for it we find it expressed in many other works of his such as *Wanderers Nachtlied*, 1 and 11, or *An den Mond* ("Füllest wieder Busch und Tal").

(2) Lenz's unfinished novel in letters, *Der Waldbruder*, "ein Pendant zu Werthers Leiden" (also partly inspired by Rousseau's *Nouvelle Heloise*) has for its hero a hermit figure who stands in strong contrast to Goethe's Erwin. Unlike Erwin, who has been scorned by his beloved, and, therefore, turns to nature and solitude to calm the turbulence of his emotions, Lenz's hermit, Herz, removes himself to the Odenwald out of an exalted and idealistic love for Gräfin Stella – there is no question of her scorning his love, and he knows her only through her letters. His lofty passion assumes the form of "Liebesschwärmerei" and he becomes a hermit primarily to preserve his ideal emotion from the sophisticated criticism of his friends in courtly society. The solitude of nature and the purity of simple living is best designed to nurture such a feeling – Herz lives rather for the ideal emotion, than for the source which inspires it. Also unlike Erwin, who, tempted by thoughts of Elmire, seeks release from a longing to return to her, Herz is (for a time, at least) thoroughly happy in the life he has chosen, and is impervious to all efforts of Rothe to coax him back.

The novel reflects Lenz's love experience with Henriette von Waldner in Weimar (cf. *Schriften*, V, p. 390, and Rosanow, *Lenz*, Chap. XII) and it is interesting to note that Lenz, like Herz, fled to the "Waldeinsamkeit" at Berka in the Thuringian forest on June 27, 1776, taking nothing with him but what he happened to be wearing (Rosanow, p. 350) – it was during his stay in the lonely forest town that he composed *Der Waldbruder*.

There is a kind of "romantische Ironie" in the novel, for, since the story is told in the letters, not only of Herz, but in those of his friends and acquaintances, we have his idealistic point of view (Honesta calls him a "Werther", and characterizes his attitude as "romantisch" – *Schriften*, p. 119) as well as the amusedly sympathetic analyses of him by Rothe and the mocking of Fräulein Schatouilleuse. Herz is, of course, Lenz, himself, while Rothe, his best friend, is Goethe. Although Herz eloquently defends his way of life, it becomes apparent through the letters of the other correspondents that he is quite pathological; he lives in a state of complete illusion

("Wahn") which is utter reality to him. As long as Herz is able to live exclusively for his ideal of love in the solitude of nature, he is safe and, in his own way, happy, but when he leaves his hermitage and involves others in his affair, his career may be expected to end tragically (pp. 135 and 138).

Rothe's final letter to Plettenberg (p. 142-145) shows that Herz's search for an ideal love was instilled in him in his youth. He had envisioned his guardian's mistress as a nymph in the *Iliad*, which he had been reading with his tutor at the age of eleven. Subsequent idealizations inspired by the heroines of Goethe and Wieland and by Klopstock's Cidli all led to disappointment. Herz would have killed himself (p. 144) but for the fact that he considered suicide a sin. Rothe, however, fears the outcome of an additional disappointment, for Herz is convinced that he has, at last, found the ideal woman in Stella, Plettenberg's fiancee.

The letters of Honesta in the third part of the novel (p. 132-139) describe the immediate background and (especially in the third letter) the motivation for Herz's hermithood. Through the machination of Frau Hohl, a homely widow who, herself, had designs on Herz, the young idealist and dreamer became acquainted with the letters of Stella (p. 134), and fell violently in love with the sublime revelation of feminine character and intellect contained in them – Stella represents a variation of the "schöne Seele" and it is with this aspect of womanhood that Herz is obsessed. Frau Hohl was also initially responsible for concealing from him the knowledge of Stella's engagement to Plettenberg, for she hoped, through his eventual disappointment, to interest Herz in herself. In his fantastic attempts to find and behold the object of his adoration, Herz had run through his money, gone into debt, and, consequently, rather than incur obligation to the Widow Hohl, he had abruptly left the city to become a hermit.

Having become a "Waldbruder", Herz finds in the solitude of nature a world and way of life commensurate with the purity and loftiness of his idealized emotion – as his name would suggest, Herz is a man of feeling, a masculine "schöne Seele". He dwells in a hut roofed with moss and leaves, and rejoices in the splendor of the surrounding country. From the mountains he looks down into a wide valley crossed by a stream, where the houses of the simple country folk are situated. Their way of life represents for Herz a pure and natural happiness – he calls them "Adamskinder" (p. 109) – and he envies them the certainty and security of the limited joys afforded by their uniform living (his reaction is similar to Werther's pleasure in observing the simple, "natural" occupations of poor villagers). The hermit figure here is eloquent statement of that Rousseauistic back-to-nature creed which became virtually a religion during the German "Sturm und Drang".

There is an unusual objectivity in Lenz's hermit, even in his "Schwärmerei", for Herz is quite conscious of the strange impression he makes on the peasants. They eye him with curiosity and it is apparent to him that they sense his homelessness – the fact that he "belongs" nowhere. Although they make fun of his lack of understanding for their ways, Herz is neither insulted nor hurt; he admits that their attitude is justified because of the manifestations in behaviour which are symptomatic of his condition and outlook upon life. As a recluse inspired by an ideal love, who finds in nature a spirit kindred in its purity, Herz considers himself indirectly comparable to Petrarch, who retired to a rocky spring near Vaucluse, and there, too, dwelt in a seclusion devoted to his feeling for Laura.[1] At any rate, Herz considers his state of mind and his adopted way of life to be in a long-standing tradition – such figures as he have always been the mark of curiosity and fun-poking.

Yet, Herz is much more averse to the mockery of his own class of society, for while the simple peasants wonder more at his manner and mode of life, members of his own social circle deride the idealized feeling for which he lives – (p. 111, bot. ff.) "Soll ich aber die Wahl haben, so ist mir der Spott des ehrlichen Landmannes immer noch Wohltat gegen das Auszischen leerer Stutzer und Stutzerinnen in den Städten."

We have observed a thread of pseudo-objectivity in Herz, but it does not affect either his evaluation of his way of life or his idealism. He is consistently able to find substantiation for his "Schwärmerei", and, although he credits the arguments of his friend, Rothe, he finds them quite inapplicable to himself (p. 117).

When he receives a penciled note from Rothe bearing only the words, "Herz, du dauerst mich!", the hermit refers the sympathy expressed by Rothe to his impoverished condition, rather than to his state of fanatical idealism (p. 110). He immediately goes on to describe his happiness in nature, but there is a melancholy strain in it which is also a source of pleasure to Herz; it is inspired by the withering shrubs of autumn and the green meadows which seem to be struggling against coming frost and snow (p. 111). It is as if nature reflected the purity and freshness of his emotion which would not survive the blighting criticism and degrading traffic of sophisticated society – p. 111) "Ich denke, es wird doch für mich auch ein Herbst einmal kommen, wo diese innere Pein ein Ende nehmen

---

[1] It is, perhaps, an interesting coincidence that the landscape of Vaucluse very closely resembles that which Herz describes – *cf.* Fredrik Wulff, *Petrarch at Vaucluse*, Lund, 1904, p. 2 and plates, and Scheffel, *Reisebilder, Ein Tag am Quell von Vaucluse*.

wird. Abzusterben für die Welt, die mich so wenig kannte, als ich sie zu kennen wünschte –, oh, welche schwermütige Wollust liegt in dem Gedanken?" He is convinced that a purely idealistic individualist of his type can never be understood by a society which does not recognize the validity of such emotion.

The strange objectivity to which we have already referred (and which, in a sense, is immanent in the hero in so far as Herz embodies any characteristics of Lenz, himself) comes to bear when Herz thinks of a concept of Rousseau – namely, that one should not demand that which does not lie within one's power to achieve; he who does, remains forever a useless, weak half-man. The hermit, Herz, sees in the concept an application to his own way of life and the motives behind it. Yet, while the idea troubles him (p. 111 mid.), it is clear that, as a recluse living in a world both real and ideal, he prefers to be useless and weak, rather than to give up his way of life and thus dull his senses to the ideal embodied in Stella (at whose birth all forces of nature were set in motion and to whose perfection heaven had combined all circumstances – p. 111).

The sublimity of the object of Herz's adoration is the prime justification, of course, for his chosen way of life, and it is important to reemphasize that it is an ideal of perfection that he sees in Gräfin Stella – not the woman, herself, outwardly. Following the moment of doubt which we have just discussed and which Herz overcomes almost in the same breath, the ecstatic recluse recalls in a panegyric the charm and splendor which the supposed Stella radiated at a masquerade. To be sure, Herz feels that an abyss lies between them (p. 111), but this feeling is only partially due to the fact that Stella's rank places her beyond his reach (cf. p. 132, mid.). Herz's attitude is that of one who worships an unapproachable ideal. The pattern of the dance had brought the assumed inspiration of his emotion to a position directly before Herz's chair, yet he was unable even to offer her a seat – (p. 112) "denn die Ehrfurcht hielt mich zurück, sie anzureden".

We realize, of course, from the subsequent letter of Fräulein Schatouilleuse to Rothe (p. 112) and from that of Rothe to Herz (p. 113 ff.) that someone had tricked Herz into identifying another young noblewoman as his beloved. The letter of Schatouilleuse reveals the source of merriment which Herz's seemingly ridiculous dedication to unreality, or illusion, provides for sophisticated society; that of Rothe (and his subsequent one – p. 115) contrasts the light manner of the "Weltmann" (satire on Goethe) in affairs of the heart with Herz's single-minded and fanatical idealism – (p. 114) "Siehst Du, so bin ich in einer beständigen Unruhe, die sich endlich in Ruhe und Wollust auflöst und dann mit einer reizenden Untreue wechselt." Rothe analyzes Herz quite properly from the point of view of his sense of reality when he calls him one of those dangerous fools who, as Shakespeare said, are incurable, because they are always able to excuse their own idiocy (p. 113). Yet Rothe fails to understand that what for him is illusion is supreme reality for Herz – it is inconceivable to him that his hermit friend should be able to dissociate the spiritual essence from the concrete individual. In spite of the fact that he is made aware of his foolish mistake at the masquerade, Herz remains constant in his lofty devotion to Stella and no coaxing or argument of Rothe can induce him to leave his hermitage; on the contrary Rothe's attitude only convinces him more firmly that he is in the right (Honesta's description of Stella justifies Herz's emotion, at least to some extent – p. 119).

Herz reveals in his answer to Rothe (p. 117 ff.) both his peculiar objectivity and the justification for the sense of a higher reality which is his alone and for which he has forsaken the brilliance of sophisticated society to bury his undeniable talents in a hermitage – (p. 117) "Sei glücklich unter Deinen leichten Geschöpfen und lass mir meine Hirngespinste. – Ich lache nicht, aber ich bin glücklicher als Ihr –. Es ist wahr, dass ich alles hier begrabe, aber eben in dieser Aufopferung findt mein Herz eine Grösse, die ihm wieder Luft macht, wenn seine Leiden zu schwer werden." The sole demand which Herz makes on life is freedom to love what he wishes with all the strength and constancy of his particular character inclination – this demand he finds fulfilled in his hermithood –

(p. 119)   "Du nicht glücklich, kümmernd Herz?
Was für Recht hast du zum Schmerz?
Ist's nicht Glück genug für dich,
Dass sie da ist, da für sich?"

The hand of Fate intervenes in the form of a freezing night which forces Herz to leave his hut, and brings him among men (p. 121). He sees his Stella in the flesh, and the intrigue over her portrait which involves Widow Hohl, Rothe, and Plettenberg leads to Herz's downfall. Although we do not possess the conclusion of the novel, we may assume a tragic ending, for Herz, who is to accompany Stella's fiance, Plettenberg, on a campaign to America, will learn of her marriage to the old colonel after it has taken place (p. 138) – this plan had been conceived by Rothe primarily to cure Herz of his illusion.

Herz embodies, as a hermit, a strange blending of fanatical idealism and individualism. In contrast to Erwin, who wishes to find peace and consolation in nature for an unhappy love, Herz finds in nature a realm of purity and simplicity conducive to complete devotion to an ideal love; hermithood is for him, as we have seen, the sole way of life in which he can indulge and preserve his emotion.

Lenz's "Waldbruder" dwells in a reality which is valid for him alone. As long as he is able to remain in solitude, and maintain the dissociation of his spiritual love from Stella, herself, as an individual, Herz enjoys peace of mind. When his destiny places him face to face with her, however, and, through his desire to possess her picture, he becomes involved with the intriguing of those whose sense of reality bears no relationship to his own, Herz and his ideal realm of experience are doomed to be shattered.

The hermit figure in Lenz's *Der Waldbruder*, then, is the very type of "romantic" or idealistic individualist whose dream world can exist only quite apart from society and, indeed, in separation from the object of his own emotion, the hermit's spiritual love possesses the purity and eternal quality of nature, itself.

(3) In Klinger's Tragedy, *Die Zwillinge*, Grimaldi, too, lives only for an ideal love, but the difference between the latter and Herz is that between day and night. Grimaldi never appears as a hermit and, although he expresses a desire to become one (p. 24), it may be assumed that he would never gain strength enough to undertake such a move. Grimaldi, like Herz, lives in devotion to an ideal love and in a world of his own. His love and the realm in which he lives, however, belong to the past, to death – they exist nowhere but in his own obsession. He might well be designated a victim of acute melancholia; as such, he acts as a foil to the unbelievably irrational raging of his friend, Guelfo, for his melancholy, which has the pallor of death, imbues the entire atmosphere of the drama with its oppressive, dark humidity – like that which pervades the air before a terrible thunder-storm.

Grimaldi's vitality (we are asked to believe that he once had strength and zest for life – p. 20) has been sapped by the death of his beloved, Juliette – Guelfo's sister (p. 22) – "Sie starb! sie starb! und da sie starb, starb Grimaldi! Alle Hoffnung und Leben entquoll meinem Herzen mit den blutigen Thränen." Ferdinando is made to bear the blame for Grimaldi's tragic experience in the past (p. 31, top and p. 22, mid.), as he is for thwarting the love of Guelfo for Kamilla during the action of the play. Grimaldi's rank was considered unsuitable for union with the family (p. 22) and Ferdinando had committed a grave wrong in belittling the melancholy knight's love for Juliette and in pressing for her marriage to a wealthy count (p. 31, top) – a marriage which was obviated by Juliette's death of a broken heart.

Grimaldi's wish to become a hermit is directed also toward Guelfo (p. 24), for, in his eyes, a fate similar to his own threatens his friend; Guelfo must look on in self-torture while Ferdinando reaps the blessing of a love which rightfully should be his – rightfully, because Guelfo, and Grimaldi, himself, embody the capacity for deep, ennobling feeling and sensitivity lacking in Ferdinando and in the society which has no insight into their sphere of experience. The expression of the wish to enter into hermithood is traceable to Grimaldi's conviction that the man of strong and idealistically emotional nature, once crushed by adversity in the form of insensitive society, can never recover himself; an inevitable tragic end awaits him, for he will exist in a living death – (p. 21) "Aber Guelfo, wenn das nun all niedergerissen ist, was uns damals trieb, wie den jungen Adler, der seine Schwingen stark fühlt, den Weg zur Sonne zu schweben – wenn das nun nicht mehr aufzuwecken ist – Lieber Guelfo, ich schein mir dem geblendeten Adler zu gleichen, der sein Leben in den Felsen austrauert." All sentiments of brighter nature, all sympathetic feeling for the fate of others, or even for his own, have been transformed in him to hatred and antipathy (p. 21, top). The desire to depart from the world, then, is motivated by revulsion toward a society which, guided by superficial standards of rank and wealth, manipulates and destroys the will to live in the feeling individual (p. 22) – "Ward ich nicht in Finsternis zurückgestossen worin ich noch immer tappe?" The longing for isolation is based equally upon a sense of frustration evoked by those (Ferdinando, the old Guelfo) who cannot grasp the suffering of the individuals whose lives they have ruined – (p. 30) "Versteht kein Mensch den Leidenden?" Grimaldi represents, therefore, a spiritual secession from life, a sort of "inner hermithood" which justifies our consideration of him in this study.

Thus, Grimaldi inhabits the dark world of his dreams, idealistically melancholy dreams of the past and of death. His hermithood would be dedicated to the expectation of death and it would be lived out in devotional sorrow – (p. 24) "Bruder, lass uns Einsiedler werden, lass uns der Welt absagen, und uns treu sterben! – Wie kann ich's, wie kannst du's ansehen? Eine härne Kutte wär des armen Grimaldi's Sache." (Guelfo is addressed as "Bruder" and included in the design of hermithood because he, alone, understands Grimaldi's love and grief for his sister, and also because, as we have said, Grimaldi foresees the tragic experience in store for his friend.)

Yet, ironically, the complete loss of strength and will to live, occasioned by his experience, would prevent Grimaldi from ever carrying out his wish to become a hermit. The fact that he exists in a dream world of living death devoted to memory of his lost love (p. 23 and p. 30, bot.) binds him most explicitly to the sombre environment of Guelfo's castle – (p. 23) "Bruder! Dir darf ich's sagen, dass mir jede Nacht ihre blasse Totengestalt erscheint, dass ich sie so kalt in meine Arme festdrücke, dass sie mir winkt, und dass sie mich nach sich zieht." Even in his despair Grimaldi is rooted to the scene of his past by his recurring ghostly rendezvous with the dead beloved.

Hermithood in Lenz's *Der Waldbruder* and the expressed desire to become a hermit in Klinger's *Die Zwillinge* represent in the instances of both Herz and Grimaldi a longing, or inner need, of the individual dwelling in an idealistic dream-reality of his own fabrication to repulse a world which endangers it. Hermithood, in both cases, is an attempt to preserve an individual reality from the infringement of a society for which that reality is quite nonexistent. The rejection of the world and the wish to do so reveal, of course, a defense mechanism against the suffering occasioned by the lack of sympathy and understanding in circles where the basis of the individual's emotional problems has no validity. (The realm of pathological melancholy and death in which Grimaldi lives is similar, although the latter does not become a hermit, to that of the hermit figure of Lenau's *Die Marionetten*, who also dwells in macabre devotion to the dead love of his gloomy past.)

(4) In Klinger's *Die Zwillinge*, Grimaldi wishes to become a hermit because his life has been shattered by the death of his beloved; he exists, as we have seen, completely in the past, in communion with the dead. Thus, his existence is utterly negative and he is, himself, without life. In Brentano's "verwilderter Roman", *Godwi*, the hermit, Werdo Senne, also dwells, to an extent, in the past; he, too, has rejected the world out of sorrow over the death of his beloved. Yet, Brentano's hermit finds consolation and inspiration in nature; his experience and his knowledge of the secrets of life through nature have made him wise and benevolent – there is little bitterness in his heart from the past – only a constant sorrow, which, however, he alleviates by imparting his knowledge of life to the young. Like Trevrizent, the hermit in *Satyros*, or even like the deceased recluse in Goethe's *Erwin und Elmire*, he represents a kind of ideal hermit – but one who embodies quite specific characteristics of German Romanticism. Of course, these are all not *religious* hermits in the churchly sense, but a sort of "lay" hermits. They neither practice religious devotions nor atone vicariously for the world's sins.

In regard to the form of the novel, H. A. Korff remarks, "– so bildet der Roman überhaupt kein Ganzes, sondern nur ein willkürliches Konglomerat von allerlei romanhaften Stoffen, die nur insofern eine Einheit bilden, als sie insgesamt erotische Stoffe sind." Youthful work though it may be, *Godwi* possesses qualities which make it more unified than a string of "Novellen" loosely connected by a common eroticism, as Korff suggests (in an otherwise illuminating chapter on the novel). It is possible to disagree with such an interpretation for various reasons; one of these is inherent in the portrayal of the hermit, Werdo Senne, whose personality is a dominant one in the first part of the novel and whose past runs like a thread through the second part, with specific clarifying references to the first – Korff does not mention Senne in his *Godwi* chapter.

We have already referred to the fact that a tragic love-experience motivates Werdo's hermithood. The second part of the novel explains this motivation through Godwi's delineation of the relationship between Joseph (Werdo Senne of part one) and Marie Wellner. Their relationship was based upon a love which would have culminated in marriage, had it not been disrupted by the force of outer circumstances. Although their love was deep and of enduring quality, it ran its course (until the death of Marie) within conventional bourgeois confines. Such a love-experience is opposed to the idealization of a free love, a boundless force of nature, which is set forth in the novel. It is only after the death of Marie that Senne's love for her assumes in hermithood the timeless depth of nature, itself.

Marie is pictured as "ein durchaus sanftes und argloses Geschöpf mit einem treuen warmen Herzen, und einem hellen Geiste, der aber meistens in der Wahl das Gute dem Schönen vorzog" (II, Ch. 19, beginning) – there is a strain of the bourgeois in the conception of her as compared with her sister, Annonciata ("ein kühneres und doch harmonischeres Gemisch von Farben ist nicht leicht denkbar"). Joseph, engaged as tutor and business assistant to Wellner, falls in love with the more conventional favorite daughter of the merchant, who blesses their betrothal with a pair of golden rings (II, Ch. 19, end). The circumstances arising out of Joseph's commercial voyage serve to break up the conventional relationship which ends in stark tragedy. Because of storms at sea (II, ch. 29, end), Joseph's return is delayed indefinitely, while Godwi (the elder) convinces the despairing Marie of her beloved's demise by destroying his letters and falsifying a death-certificate. Consequently, Marie is persuaded by her ailing father to marry Godwi, to whom she bears a son (Godwi, the younger) – thus the catastrophe, which Joseph's homecoming occasions, and which motivates his hermithood, ripens.

Through separation from him, Marie's love deepens and becomes endless longing. On one of her accustomed evening walks with her child along the harbor, Marie hears the voice of Joseph from an approaching ship, and sees him looking toward her through a telescope.[1] Overcome, probably, by her sense of guilt and by the longing which can never be fulfilled, she plunges with the infant Godwi (later rescued) into the sea (II, ch. 27, end) – she breaks the

---

[1] cf. Herder, *Stimmen der Völker in Liedern, Das Mädchen am Ufer*, which presents a similar scene, (including the "Kaufmannsgestalt"), one which may have influenced Brentano, who was surely familiar with it.

confines of the conventional love of her past through her act, and becomes "das steinerne Bild der Mutter". This statue of Marie poised with the child in her arms becomes an eternal reminder of his guilt to the elder Godwi, who had it placed outside the window of his lonely dwelling (II, ch. 18, id.), and it represents, at the same time, Joseph's last view of her – it is this sight and conception of Marie which accompanies him into his retreat. By her act, Marie embodies the death of constricting, bourgeois emotion, and becomes for the hermit, Werdo Senne, the very symbol of an eternally pervading, depersonalized love, a force of nature –

(1, p. 140)   "Wenn die Liebe aus den Sternen
              Niederblicket auf die Erde,
              Und dein Liebstes Lieb begehrte,
              Muss dein Liebstes sich entfernen."

(This interpretation of Marie's transition from conventional love to an embodiment of a boundless love inherent in nature is substantiated by the comparison of the painting of Marie before her death with the statue (II, ch. 20, end). Of the painting, the poet, Marie, says, "Ich habe noch nirgends ein häusliches Gemählde im Ideal gesehen, dies ist es, Friede." Of his mother's portraits in both painting and statue, Godwi replies, "Dies ist sie, ziehen Sie von diesem Bilde bis zum steinernen Bilde eine Linie, so haben Sie das Unglück meiner Mutter ermessen.")

After the death of Marie, Joseph suffered a transitory spell of insanity (II, ch. 27 end). Following his recovery, however, the knowledge of what had transpired during his absence produced in him a terrible solemnity which induced him to enter into hermithood – Godwi's reference to a second marriage of Joseph (II, 30) and the death of the second wife as an additional cause of his hermithood may well be attributed to an attempt to lift a measure of guilt from his father's memory.

From Ottilie's letter to Joduno (I, p. 48 ff.) we learn that Werdo lives plunged in sorrow and in longing for death which shall reunite him with Marie as well as with the second wife (cf. above) – "Ich werde bald deine Mutter, mein treues, edles Weib, wieder sehen, ich werde auch Jene wieder sehen, die mein Wiedersehn tödtete." Werdo finds happiness in this longing and conviction, for, as he says, without it he would scarcely be capable of even the wish to die. His sorrow and longing for death find expression and consolation in the songs which he sings to the accompaniment of his harp (Werdo is an echo of Goethe's "Harfner" in *Wilhelm Meister*, as are also many of the other characters and themes in the work). The relationship of the romantic conception of moonlight and night to the death-longing is revealed as the soft rays of the moon fill the chamber with their mild light, and inspire Werdo to take his harp – (I. p. 50) "Es war mir, als habe er sein Lied an dem Monde angezündet, es war so rein, so hell, und doch so mild, was er sang" – thus, here, the conception of night and death-longing are synthesized in Werdo's music, embodied in art. The tragic experience of his past assumes a uniquely positive aspect in Senne's hermithood, for it is transformed into his gift of song.

Werdo Senne dwells in a hermitage which he has constructed in the ruins of an ancient castle, Reinhardstein (I, p. 79 ff.). Here, he secludes himself with his daughter, Ottilie, and the foundling boy, Eusebio (a male echo of Mignon) who had been committed to his care by Lady Hodefield. He had hidden himself among these ruins, he informs Godwi, that men might not hear his laments and that he might not hear their lies (I, p. 79). In his care, the two children, Ottilie and Eusebio, have bloomed like flowers, in intimacy with nature and with an inexpressible, instinctive understanding of its pervading force; they, too, have acquired Werdo's gift of song – even their inspiration is identical with that of their father – (I, p. 137) "Leise, wie ein Lied des Danks, zündete sich Eusebio's Stimme am Mond an" – (cf. previous quotation).

Godwi is at once aware of the melancholy peace in which Senne lives; the suffering, which has been transformed into a deep understanding of nature and a longing to be united with it, lends the hermit an aspect of solitary greatness in the eyes of the young visitor (I, p. 80); he does not speak readily with strangers and there is in his bearing, alone, a power which silences the lips of others. About him is an aura of serene peace, not unlike that which a feeling man experiences in the stillness of the evening after a full and tiring day.

Werdo Sonne's principal source of consolation is his harp; he is accustomed to sitting for hours beneath a lonely oak where he lifts his voice in songs of enchanting power – a power derived from the longing ("Sehnsucht") inherent in them for something that he alone knows (I, p. 81). To Godwi it seems that in Werdo's songs lies the key to his suffering, for the hermit rests his forehead upon the harp as if it were the arm of a comforting friend (I, p. 83).

When the hermit becomes convinced that his young visitor, Godwi, possesses an instinctive sympathy for his sorrow, he explains that his solitary life is characterized by deep unity with all that lives about him (I, p. 140). Again he raises his voice in song and, although the theme of Marie's death is its ouverture, the poem reveals in its development the joy and peace of eternal unity in nature and God which is the fruit of his tragic experience –

(1. p. 142)   "Ich sinke ewig unter
                Und steige ewig auf,

> Und blühe stets gesunder
> Aus Liebes-Schoos herauf.
> Das Leben nie verschwindet,
> Mit Liebesflamm und Licht
> Hat Gott sich selbst entzündet
> In der Natur Gedicht."

In harmony with nature, the hermit dwells in the realm of eternal love and longing; only nature is able to offer him comfort in his suffering and it has taught him its language, song (I, p. 143 – "und lebe wie Natur, in freien und ungebundenen Tönen"). The aspect of the eternal revealed to the hermit in nature is a quality felt, or lived ("erlebt", perhaps, "geahnt"); it is the very antithesis of knowledge – (I, p. 144) "denn alles Wissen ist der Tod der Schönheit, die in uns wohnet".

Thus, the hermit, Werdo Senne, also performs an educational function (as do the solitaries in *Heinrich von Ofterdingen*, *Eine Meerfahrt*, and *Oberon* – chapter IV of this study), for his experience has formative influence not only upon the lives of Ottilie and Eusebio, but upon Godwi, who absorbs the hermit's conception of nature as eternal love and longing, as the only ultimate way of life –

(1, p. 146) "Es stürzen bald des alten Glaubens Götzen
Zieht die Natur mich so mit Liebe an.
O süsser Tod, in Liebe neu geboren,
Bin ich der Welt, doch sie mir nicht verloren."

As an eventual result of Senne's teaching, Godwi, himself, retires to the solitude of his "Eremitage" in the second part of the novel.

Although Senne starts in horror when Godwi, overcome with enthusiasm, addresses him as "Vater!" (I, p. 146), his behaviour is due to shock, rather than to any lasting bitterness from the past. The arrival of Godwi, (the son he might have had) revives in the hermit the initial pain of Marie's death and betrayal, which he had transcended in hermithood (I, p. 144). The nobility of character inherent in Senne's suppression of such bitterness is revealed in his first letter to Lady Hodefield – (I, p. 78) "Der ist kein edler Mensch, der sich nicht freut der Liebe im Arme seines Nebenbuhlers, und der ist ein niedriger Mensch, der sich nicht freut des Werths der Kinder, deren Vater er hätte seyn können." The same nobility and lack of bitterness is evident in Senne's reconciliation with the elder Godwi, the perpetrator of his greatest misfortune (II, ch. 31, p. 457).

In Werdo Senne's hermithood there runs also the theme of the relationship between art and madness. Godwi feels that "Wahnsinn" wages a continuous struggle for control of the hermit's spirit (I, p. 147) – Madness is the unfortunate brother of Poetry, and is often thrust aside in life. The stark realities in the world, however, hinder the flight of Poetry, while Madness, in his frequent victories over the adversities in life, bears his prize aloft to the very gods. The hermit, Senne, as we have seen, possesses an instinctive understanding for the eternal power of nature, and, in hermithood, his own longing has become harmonized with it. This universally instinctive understanding of a profounder sense of life in nature, this phantasy ("Wahnsinn"), creates its own reality – the fertile soil which gives birth to the purest song. (This conception of the relationship between "Wahnsinn" and art is clearly allied to Hoffmann's "serapiontisches Prinzip" and similar to a theme in Wackenroder's *Der nackte Heilige*).

As a hermit, Werdo Senne embodies a supreme wisdom and kindly benevolence, the fruits of a tragic experience transformed through profound insight into nature; the longing for reunion with the dead betrothed was translated in him into a longing for union with nature, the element of eternal love (and, in this universal respect, all longing is for Werdo Senne "Todessehnsucht").

We have also seen that the natural expression of this longing is song, the language of nature, itself. Senne performs an educational function through the transmission of his "Weltanschauung" to Godwi and through his influence upon Eusebio and Ottilie, who represent for Godwi the hermit's insight into life become flesh. Werdo's concept of the world of nature as the realm of universal, eternal love and longing lends depth and perspective to the criticism of the novel as a whole.

Werdo Senne's hermithood, therefore, is a positive way of life, for it is a triumph over the tragedy and bitterness of his past, an entry into a richer, eternal aspect of life and art. The aged man characterizes his life as a hermit most aptly in the conclusion of his letter to Lady Hodefield – (I, p. 78) "Sonderbar ist das Gewebe meines Lebens gewesen, ein Geheimnis liegt über ihm, keine Staatenverhältnisse, keine sogenannten Wichtigkeiten, Menschenliebe und Duldung haben ihm das Siegel eiserner Verschwiegenheit aufgedrückt. Und das alles wird sich um uns drehen, diese Freudensphäre wird auf meinem Grabe stehen wie der Fuss des Regenbogens, unter dem in meinem Vaterlande ein freundlicher Aberglaube Schätze wähnt."

(5) The hermithood of Werdo Senne represented a triumph over the tragedy and suffering of his past; in isolation, that pain was transformed into a deep understanding of life through nature, which found its expression in song – all "Todessehnsucht" became a desire for union with eternal nature (as, also, in Kerner, *Die Heimatlosen*, Novalis', *Ofterdingen*, and Hölderlin's *Hyperion*). In this longing and in the expression of it, the hermit found a sort of peace. In the

case of Walter, the hermit-hero of Annette von Droste-Hülshoff's youthful "Epos", quite the reverse is true. It is, like her mature poem, *Das Vermächtnis des Arztes*, to an extent, an "allegory of man as such, doomed to guilt and suffering beyond his comprehension or desert" (Walter Silz – *Problems of "Weltanschauung" in the Works of Annette von Droste-Hülshoff, P.M.L.A.*, 1949, p. 681). In *Walter*, too, the force of evil overpowers the individual and, although the hero seeks peace and consolation in solitude, the tragedy of his love experience continually tortures him, and makes of his hermithood an agonizing purgatory (cf. previous reference – p. 693).

The poetess suggests the eventual subjection of her hero to the dark forces of fate through her delineation of his family background. The birth of Theatilde occasions the death of her own mother, which, in turn, breaks her father's heart (*Werke*, Bd. 4, p. 140). His despairing end casts its shadow over the wedding of Theatilde to Alhard (p. 148) and the union of the tender, angelic girl with the fierce robber-knight symbolizes, in itself, the hopeless plight of innocence in conflict with overwhelmingly sinister forces in life –

(p. 149)   "Hat je dem Weih' die Taube wohlgewollt?
             Ist wohl der Hinde in des Löwen Höhle?"

Theatilde wilts like an uprooted flower, while Walter, the fruit of this unequal alliance, is destined from birth, as it were, to suffer the painful experience of life's duality, from which even hermithood brings no release.

The "Epos" has the form of a "Rahmenerzählung," and the first canto introduces the hermit, Walter, who inhabits a rocky cave in the depths of a pine forest. The succeeding cantos disclose Walter's family background (to which we have already referred) and his own life prior to hermithood, while the sixth and final canto describes his departure from the world, and reverts to the opening scene.

The dim light of the moon through the dark pines reveals in the cell of the recluse the meaningful objects which surround him – a skull, symbol of death and of the transitory quality of all things, a crucifix, a suit of armor on the wall (cf. Ofterdingen), which is a dumb reminder of its owner's former life, and the empty bed of foliage. The hermit's restlessness, his lack of inner peace, are apparent from his nocturnal wandering, and, when he appears out of the darkness, shrouded in nightly mist, it is as if he were emerging cloaked in his own melancholy past (p. 134). The pallor of his face and his wavering steps disclose also the mental anguish which characterizes Walter's lonely existence; though still young, his beauty has withered, and the traces of suffering in his features indicate that he has been unable to conquer the pain which has accompanied him to his lonely retreat (p. 135). The armor which he had worn as a knight reminds him of former joyous days, but his weakened arm is unable to support its weight and it clatters to the floor of the cave – a symbol of the blight which had come over his exuberant youth. His eyes avoid the silent witness of knighthood, but even in prayer Walter cannot find the peace of God, for natural memories insist upon their rights, and pierce the calm of his devotion – as long as man is bound to earthly life, he cannot avail himself of divine consolation –

(p. 137) "Wer deine Lust begehrt, du Herrscher gross,
Den darf kein sinnlich Freudenbild mehr rühren –."

The thought of his dead beloved recurrently interposes itself between his struggling spirit and the peace it seeks – Walter clutches her pictured image to his heart, not that of the Virgin and Child, and bursts into tears of anguish and frustration. The young hermit's effort to attain spiritual calm is doomed to heart-rending failure –

(p. 138) "O Jüngling, einer heillos finstern Macht
Ist dein zerstörtes Leben hingegeben –."

The dark power which is meant here, however, is not specifically that which, in Walter, ties him to memories of earthly joy and tragedy, but rather some obscure, cosmic power of destiny which renders the individual a helpless sufferer in circumstances with which he cannot cope.

In the dream which impels Walter to seek out Alba's dwelling place on the following morning, there is a slight forboding of tragedy to come, as well as a suggestion of the sinister power which motivates it. Walter is embraced in his sleep, at first, by an angel and then –

(p. 157) "Da sind die süssen Züge all verrückt,
Ein fremdes Antlitz lächelt auf den Armen."

The vision disappears and the entire choir of angels assumes the features of the beloved Alba – thus this dark cosmic force injects itself into the destiny of the individual. With graying dawn, Walter sets out to find the angelic maiden, whose love and tragic death shall be his constant memories in isolation.

The figure of Balduin, Alba's hermit father, represents an antithesis to the eventual hermithood of Walter, for the aged recluse has been able to purge from his mind all thoughts and influences of wordly life. He dwells with his daughter in a tiny hut secluded in a forest glade remote from the world; the hut is situated on a brook, and is idyllically surrounded by grape-vines and jasmine blossoms (p. 158) – the atmosphere breathes the very essence of peace and innocence. Balduin, a former resident of the imperial capital, had inherited vast wealth from his family, yet his disposition was inclined toward loftier riches of the spirit – (p. 160) "Ich hatte höhern Fahnen zugeschworen." He had felt the splendor of the world to be a burden weighing down his spirit, which, even then, longed for solitude and harmony with God –

(p. 160)   "O Kreis der Alten, Flamme in der Nacht,
Du reine in sich selbst entglühte Leuchte!
Du warst es, deren stolzer Geistespracht
Sich demutsvoll mein schwaches Sinnen neigte."

Balduin feels gratitude for the God-given strength which enabled him to bear up under the weight of vain "Erdenglück." The luxury in which he had been obliged to live drew swarms of unwelcome guests about him and he resented the intrusion upon his privacy and the disturbance to his natural desire for spiritual peace and meditation (p. 160). Since his wealth was a curse and impediment to his peace of mind, it was with a sense of relief that he looked upon the charred ruins of his palace, which was gutted by a night fire through the intervention of some happy fate – releasing him forever from the confines of wordly vanity. This loss sufficed to let plans of long standing come to fulfillment. Three lines sum up Balduin's ideal of existence –

(p. 161)   "Nicht reich, doch sorglos, herrschend nicht, doch frei,
Nur der Natur und ihrem Zepter treu,
Am klaren Born der Alten mich zu letzen."

(The "Alten," to whom Balduin refers in this and the previous quotation, are, perhaps, the early Christian hermits who gave up all earthly goods to serve God through isolated devotion – this hermit is motivated by a desire similar, in many respects, to that of Lessing's "Klosterbruder.")

Hermithood is, therefore, the fulfillment of Balduin's most fervent wishes –

(p. 161)   "Erfüllt sind meine Wünsche; seh' ich nicht
Ein kleines Eden rings um mich erblühen?
Und drinnen glänzt, ein holdes Liebeslicht,
Mein einzig Kind in frischer Jugend Glühen."

He and Alba live in an "Eden" of original love and innocence in nature; the aged recluse spends his hours in cultivating his daughter's spirit in accordance with his ideal of life (like Werdo and Ottilie). Thus, Alba, as the product of her father's way of life, becomes the embodiment of natural innocence and love – a moving symbol of the original state of man. Through her (and through the mingled characteristics of his inheritance, as we have seen), this ideal takes firm roots in Walter's heart, but it is doomed to be crushed by the fatal forces which subject it to conflict with the incompatible influences of the outer (here, knightly,) world.

The ideals of knightly glory push their way into Walter's life, decisively and openly in conflict with the new-found love for the angelic Alba. He is to add his fame to that of his fathers by taking part in the crusade (p. 164), and is to receive as reward, upon his return, the hand of Cäcilia (p. 16), daughter of the old knight, Ebbo – she is the essence of courtly coquetry (p. 167) and of insidious pride and jealousy. The incipient conflict of incompatible forces in Walter's soul is indicated by the mixed emotions of his reaction to this news –

(p. 165) "Wie auf der Freude Glut im Antlitz ging,
Ihn dann als lichte Flamme hell umfing –
Und nun in blassen Leichenduft verschwommen."

When Walter takes leave of Balduin and Alba (p. 171), the young knight makes show of his zeal to serve God; this holy service in the crusade must come before friendship. The old hermit, however, recognizes his embarrassed pretentiousness, and, perceiving the armlet given to Walter by the false Cäcilia, lays his finger upon the embroidered figure of Amor –

(p. 171) "Glaubt mir's, dies ist der Eu'ren Fahnenzeichen!"– Balduin clearly sees the duality which holds sway in the young man's soul, and this incident is a portent of the fearful psychic struggle which marks Walter's hermithood. The knight departs, his heart divided between desire for knightly glory (worldly vanity) and thoughts of Alba – but it is the green ivy sprig, the innocent maiden's pledge and a symbol of natural purity, which acts as a talisman to guarantee Walter's safe return (p. 172), and not the artificial favor of Cäcilia (a symbol of superficiality and faithlessness – p. 170).

The death of Balduin, of which the young knight learns upon his return (p. 176), followed a spell of madness – brought on, no doubt, by the realization that his daughter's attachment to Walter dooms her to a hopeless lot. His dying words envision the tragic end of innocence and purity when it becomes exposed to the sinister forces of the world –

(p. 177) "Mein Kind, wie hilflos lass ich dich zurück!
Du arm, für diese Welt verdorbnes Leben!"

In Balduin, the hermit figure is interpreted as possessing a deep insight into life because of his intimate rapport with the natural and divine elements – thus, he is more sensitive to forces antipathetic to his way of life, such as those to which Walter is subject and which he had been able to observe in the young knight on the occasion of his departure for the crusade.

The anxiety of the dying hermit concerning the fate of his daughter proves to be visionary, for the hellish, destructive forces about Walter, embodied in his father, Alhard, and in his jealous betrothed, Cäcilia, combine on the misty night of Alba's rendezvous with her beloved to snuff out her life (p. 181-183) – "hellish" is the proper word, for Alhard's followers seem to serve "dem Höllenreiche" (p. 181) and "die grause Höllenlache" of Cäcilia (p. 183) is the last sound to fall upon the fainting Walter's ear after the deed.

Following his father's burial and the repayment of those robbed and oppressed by Alhard, Walter seeks out Verenus, the hermit-monk, whose peace in God had impressed and consoled him at the death-bed (p. 186). While he awaits the arrival of Verenus, the crucifix in the quiet cell seems to instill a divinely inspired tranquillity into his heart; the young man resolves to reject the empty world, for he has no further demands on life –

(p. 191) "In stiller Klause schweigt des Busens Toben-." Yet, Verenus' insight into Walter's problem reveals his practical wisdom – hermithood is not for the young, before whom the furure is only beginning to unfold –

(p. 192) "Schlagt nicht in Fesseln dieses heisse Herz,
Sonst, fürcht' ich, weint Ihr einst mit herbem Schmerz
Der Welt zu lieblich lockende Gestade."

As we observed at the start of our discussion, solitude brings no peace to the young hermit, for he brings with him into his retreat the "Dämon" which motivated the tragic conflict of forces in his past and which now, in Walter's case, remains to stir ceaselessly the torment of these forces in his soul. At the outset of the poem, the poetess tells us that Walter's life is subject to an unholy dark power (p. 138); the conclusion restates the fact that the world and memory of the beloved do not, of themselves, withhold spiritual calm (p. 194) –

"Es ist ein furchtbar Etwas, das sich müht,
Sich zwischen ihn und seinen Gott zu stellen –."

It is, rather, a force which motivates the dualism in life; this same fateful power stirs up tormenting recollections of the tragic events which grew out of it. Walter, as a hermit, is the sum of all the conflicts in his past over which he had no control, but which have crushed him – denying to him for the length of his earthly days the calm of spirit in God which he so feverishly desires.

The hermit theme plays a role on three levels in Annette's poem, as we have seen. Balduin is the hermit by natural inclination. He holds the world's goods and vanities in contempt, and longs only to devote himself to God and to a life in nature – peace in God is for him (as for Lessing's "Klosterbruder") an impossibility in the world of men. It is interesting to note that Annette (like Lessing) turns, as did her romantic prececessors also, to the world of the middle ages for the setting of her narrative poem; earthly life was considered in those times (at least in religious circles) to be specifically a preparation for eternity. As a hermit, Balduin lives in an "Eden" of his own making, and rears his daughter, Alba, in the purity and innocence of nature. His hermithood proves to be no solution in one sense, however, for innocence and purity are doomed to suffering through contact with the forces of the outer world. These he recognizes in Walter, and dies despairing of his daughter's future.

Verenus embodies wisdom commensurate with his age and experience (although we learn nothing specific of his background); he knows that hermithood can be of no avail as a solution for youth (as do Novalis's Hohenzollern and Eichendorff's Don Diego) upon whom the shackles of earthly life still hang. His warning to Walter proves to be precisely valid. It is possible that Verenus' way of life has brought him the peace of God, for he belongs to the clerus, and is a venerable man, whose ties are stronger to death than to life – his understanding of Alhard's dying gestures (p. 187) might also suggest this.

To Walter, as we have seen, isolation can bring no peace. In him, hermithood illustrates the extent to which the individual can be tortured and crushed by forces beyond his control and understanding.

(6) In Lenau's *Die Marionetten*, the hermit also dwells in solitude devoted to grief over a tragic bygone love and his only source of consolation lies in the recounting of its gruesome history. Unfortunately the poem was conceived during a period in which Lenau was undergoing a crisis in his creative process (cf. Errante, *Lenau*, p. 155 ff. –) and his "Nachtstück" (inspired by those of Hoffmann, and composed in the terza rima of Chamisso) is a frequently mechanically constructed horror tale which does not lend the hermit characters (Marie's father is also a sort of recluse) much depth.

The poet uses the effects of nature to provide atmosphere for his verse-tale and to suggest the spiritual plight of his hermit-narrator. The dark and rocky environment of the hermitage and the sense of foreboding in the air are descriptive of the state in which the hermit lives and of the gruesome recollections of the past which oppress him – the nature of the hermitage distinguishes the character of the hermit (as, also, in the instances of Walter, Balduin, and Werdo Senne). The tuft of lamb's wool clinging to a briar, the bloodstain underfoot, and the vulture lazily veering off to his lonely nest (Lenau, *Sämtliche Werke*, Bd. I – 1. 1320 ff.) indicate the stark tragedy which had befallen not only the hermit, but Count Robert and his daughter, the innocent Maria. The threatening darkness of the gorge through which the wanderer descends to the abode of the recluse – (1. 1339) "Die dunkle Wiege der Melancholei" – and the roar of thunder and flashes of lightning along the rocky cliffs intimate the morbid dedication to death and sorrow which characterize the hermit, who (like Grimaldi and, in a sense, like Walter) inhabits the nether regions of an ever-present past – (1.1345) "Wo murmelnd Nacht und Tod sich Treue schwören." The unusual pallor of the hermit's face and the strange light which hovers about him (1. 1353 ff.) in the storm make an impression upon the approaching wanderer, which would suggest the state of pathological suffering gnawing at the soul of the recluse.

Lenau's setting, like that of Annette, is medieval, and his hermit, like Walter, is a former knight whose grievous memories are kept fresh by the portrait of the beloved adorning his cave (1. 1377 ff.) –

(1. 1379 ff.) "Drauf wies er hin und sprach: Ich denke dein!
Und plötzlich stürzten Tränen ihm hervor.
Auf seinen Zügen lag ein tiefes Leid,
Wie er im teuren Bilde sich verlor."

In youth he had followed Count Robert through battle (1. 1443 ff.) and, upon returning from these glorious feasts of arms with the old nobleman, he fell deeply in love with the latter's daughter, the beauteous Maria, who did not requite his feeling – indeed she was scarcely aware of it (1. 1462 ff.). The young knight, however, suppressed his desire even then, and resigned himself to the bitter pleasure of unfulfilled passion (1. 1461). This attitude discloses the strain of resignation inherent in the youth of the hermit which is transformed in him after Maria's death into the doubtful consolation found in his retelling of the story and in the implied self-torture which characterizes his isolation.

Count Robert, himself, embodies in his hermithood several motifs which we have observed in other figures. He is, of course, an old knight, saddened by the deaths of those close to him (1. 1407), who withdraws from the world with his daughter (like Werdo Senne and Balduin). She is the sole comfort of his declining years. Like Senne, he makes his abode in the ruins of an ancient castle – here, the decayed seat of his ancestors (1. 1425 ff.). The theme of the weary warrior whose span of life is almost empty, and, therefore, has the right to peaceful seclusion in preparation for death –

((1. 1414)   "Geschieden von der Welt bewegten Scharen
Hat sich sein Herz, das nur den Frieden sucht,
Des Glückes letzte Spur sich zu bewahren –"

is strikingly similar to those in *Oberon, Ofterdingen,* and *Meerfahrt.*

In a sense, too, like Annette's hermit, Balduin, Count Robert's tranquil solitude – and with it his life – is destroyed by the fate of his daughter. Maria represents purity and natural innocence protected by isolation from sullying influences of the world, as did Alba – although these motifs are not nearly so extensively developed in Lenau's poem – (1. 1422 ff.)

> "An Schönheit wunderbar, an tiefer Güte,
> War selige Genüg ihr stilles Leben,
> Dass sie den Abend ihres Vaters hüte."

The robbery of Maria's peace and innocence by the byronic wanderer (1. 1485-1496), Lorenzo (cf. also *Werke*, Bd. X, p. 297), and her death of a broken heart plunge the aged hermit-Count into the madness which culminates in a gruesome revenge upon both Lorenzo and his son Antonio – noteworthy is the association of "Wahnsinn" with the heartbroken hermit – (1. 1573 – "Die Nacht des Wahnsinns schlug sich um sein Haupt") as, also, in the case of Werdo and Balduin (all three are hermit-father types).

We learn (1. 1556 ff.) from the hermit-narrator, that he had fled again into battle to avoid witnessing Lorenzo's seduction of Maria; yet his heart is consumed by jealousy and pain at a distance. Although he tells us that he had received the news of Maria's betrayal and death, we do not learn of the specific circumstances of his withdrawal, for he makes an immediate transition to Count Robert's madness and vengeful search for Lorenzo. It may be surmised that madness had come over him, too, and, as we know, he retired to a cave in the dark gorge overlooking the castle ruins and site of the entire tragic and gruesome history. Lenau's hermit does not seclude himself out of any desire to seek peace, but rather to indulge his obsession for reliving the past – to finish his story on the scene in which it took place, he leads the wanderer before the ruins of Count Robert's castle.

The sole motivation for life in Lenau's hermit is his desire, as we have said, to reexperience the past which has broken his life; this is evident, too, in his drive to tell his story, to bring it to life for the wanderer (the "Vermittler" of a horror tale in a manner similar to that of the monk in Grillparzer's *Das Kloster bei Sendomir*). Once he has concluded it, he has no further interest in the listener, but leaves him swooning from horror. Before dawn, he has disappeared, with the obsession for which he lives, into the bleak, dark mountain gorge.

In Lenau's poem, as in Annette's, the principal hermit figure represents the individual broken by the sinister forces of fate, but there is, after all, more of Grimaldi in the nature of Lenau's recluse, who does not seek calm of spirit (like Walter). The hermit-narrator of *Die Marionetten* is an utterly pathological figure clinging in hermithood to the scene and motifs of a gruesome past – he finds his only release in the indulgence of this obsession and in retelling its history.

We have observed the frequent theme of madness in connection with hermits in this part of the study – in Balduin, whose fate as a hermit-father was comparable to Count Robert's, in Werdo-Senne, another hermit-father (the conception of madness and art was a theme in his hermithood) as well as in Lenau's hermit-narrator. We may add that, in a remote sense, there is in the hermit-narrator of *Die Marionetten* a suggested tie between the effectiveness of story-telling and the madness of the hermit. The ability to recreate so intensely the horror of his past for the listener is in direct proportion to the degree of obsession which forces the hermit to relive it – whether coincidental or not, this conception of madness is certainly reminiscent of that in Hoffman's *Serapion*.

B. This brief subdivision in the second part of our study concerns itself with three hermit figures characterized specifically by their madness.

(1) In Klinger's novel, *Fausts Leben, Thaten und Höllenfahrt*, the devil, Leviathan, commits himself in the pact with Faust to disclosing the hypocrisy, superficiality, and perverse nature of man (p. 170 ff.). The hermit is singled out as the apotheosis of virtue, simplicity, and devotion to God; through his destruction, the devil wishes to demonstrate to Faust the sham which underlies all apparent reverence and faith among men; there is no virtue so constant that it will not ultimately succumb to temptation.

The attack upon the hermit's morality is a revolting parallel to the temptation of St. Anthony; the hermit succumbs to the temptation to which he is, perhaps, most vulnerable because of his isolation. He succumbs, however, to the temptation only after he has been driven literally mad through Leviathan's conjuration of a seductress in the guise of a female pilgrim – in reality, a hellish apparition. Even though the devil's design to transform the holy man into a crazed murderer succeeds, the disgusted reader is rather more likely to share the view of the peasants who revere the hermit's bones (p. 189) – that the recluse is actually a martyr, not a poseur (like Lessing's hermit in Chapter II of this study). Although it is clearly not Klinger's intention, the violent and luridly described temptation of the hermit is likely to arouse the reader's sympathy for him.

The hermit whom Leviathan subjects to his experiment appears to Faust (p. 184) to be the very ideal of a recluse; in his heart there is the peace which is evident in the composure of his features and Faust is led to believe that the hermit's hope and faith make him a far more enviable man than he who made the pact with the devil. In his hospitality to the two strangers, the hermit obeys the tradition associated with his way of life; he is happy to minister to all who may come to him and his lonely life is not spent in completely useless inactivity (p. 184) – "Derjenige, der dem Himmel lebt, darf der gefährlichen Ruhe nicht pflegen." The mildness of his temperament does not permit him to grow angry at Leviathan's taunts; he reveals his humility when the devil accuses him of weakness, of fear of temptation (p. 186) – to the challenge that struggle and temptation are the triumphs of sainthood, the hermit humbly replies, "Der Herr hat recht; aber nicht alle sind Heilige." The hermit, therefore, is precisely what he appears to be – a man who has fled the world because of its temptations (like Simplicissimus) to devote himself to God and to save his soul (p. 187) – "Es ist eine sündige Welt, in der wir leben, und weh' ihr, wenn tausende nicht in die Einsamkeit eilten, ihr Leben dem Gebet weihten, um die Rache des erzürnten Himmels von dem Haupt der Sünder abzuwenden."

It is, in a sense, through the charity of his office that the seductress is able to reach the godly man; she seems to seek refuge with him from the advances of Leviathan. Thus, his senses already inflamed, the hermit falls prey to the temptress (p. 188), who so shatters his entire being that he becomes a madman prepared to murder the two guests to whom he had offered his hospitality.

Crushed by realization of his entanglement with the hellish powers, the hermit faints, and perishes in the flames which release him from his ghastly plight. Faust's accurate suspicion of the devil's intent prior to the hermit's horrible psychic struggle actually interprets most exactly what transpires (p. 185) – "und du wirst die Sinne dieses Gerechten so verwirren, dass er Thaten unternimmt, die seinem Herzen fremd sind."

It is difficult to say much more of Klinger's hermit than that he is traditional in conception (a clerical figure, however) – a refugee from the evils of the reformation world, who wishes to save his soul by devoting his life entirely to God. Yet, because of his isolation and asceticism, he is vulnerable to evil forces – extreme asceticism and godliness are transformed by temptation to mad voluptuosity. The figure of the hermit represents the ultimate virtue and reverence in his ascetic isolation from the world of sinful men; he is, therefore, made the goal of an attack which designs to prove that all human faith and devotion is without constancy or substance. Hermithood, then, provides no absolute peace in God, for even in isolation the hermit (as in *Walter*) is sought out and martyred by forces of evil in the world. Such an interpretation, to be sure, runs counter to Klinger's actual intent. The author wishes to convey the fact (as did Lessing) that there are some blackguards even among hermits – madness here consists of sexual desire rampant, overriding every scruple.

The same attitude of contempt prevails, though more concisely and violently expressed, toward the Sicilian hermit, Martarillo, whom the great King Louis of Sicily visits (p. 252 ff.). The mighty monarch reveres the hermit as a holy man, begging him to grant long life and health – the hermit is described as (p. 253) a fool who has lived on the peak of a cliff from his fourteenth to his fortieth year, torturing his body by fasting and denying his spirit all nourishment ("aber der Schein des Heiligen bedeckte den Dummkopf und er sah bald die Fürsten wie den Pöbel zu seinen Füssen"). It is, for Faust, a supreme irony in life that such a creature commands the respect even of rulers, and thus, perhaps, exerts in his madness a decisive influence upon the world.

(2) In Wackenroder's *Ein wunderbares morgenländisches Märchen von einem nackten Heiligen*, the relationship of art (here, music) to madness as a theme connected with the hermit is developed in a manner basically different from the conception in Werdo Senne (Wackenroder's tale pre-dates Brentano's *Godwi*); here, the treatment is, to an extent, allegorical – a treatment more compatible, also, with the "Märchen" technique.

For Wackenroder (as for many other successive Romantics) the Orient is the land of mystery and profoundly irrational truths. His hermit figure is one of the original Dervishes inhabiting the eastern wastes. A kind of sacred madness is associated with these solitaries, which sets them apart from other men; they are considered to be of essentially supernatural nature, and, as such, are objects of worship (while in philistine Europe they would be considered merely insane).

The hermit of the "Märchen" dwells in a rocky cave by a little river; how he came there, or why, no one knows – the original circumstances underlying his hermithood are as mysterious as, in a sense, his eventual departure from life. What characterizes this hermit, however, is the particular nature of his madness – his obsession with the rushing wheel of time (p. 157) which roars in his ears, and whirls without interruption – "wie sich mit Brausen, mit gewaltigem Sturmwindsausen das fürchterliche Rad drehte und wieder drehte, das bis an die Sterne und hinüber reichte." Its revolutions border directly on the spheres of eternal harmony. Of all men, only the wretched hermit is aware of its fateful turning; in fear that it may cease, he becomes the victim of enraged, frustrated anxiety and his solitude is marked by frenzied torment – peace is unknown to him. Thus, the recluse becomes a kind of allegorical embodiment of man, in the last analysis, alone, attempting to master the single great force, time, the furious rhythms of which confine and regulate all earthly existence.

Wackenroder's hermit represents in his isolation an extreme individualism which is obsessed with the problem of time – a problem conceived in terms of the maddening rhythms of the wheel, and one which grips the individual, never the group.

As the hermit weakens in his strenuous attempts to master and control the wheel, a terrible fear seizes him, for he often senses an impulse to interrupt the perpetual revolutions by relinquishing his grasp (p. 159). Often on moonlit nights, he weeps bitterly, because all other activity in life has been denied him – "dass das Sausen des mächtigen Zeitrades ihm nicht Ruhe lasse, irgend etwas zu tun, zu handeln, zu wirken und zu schaffen." His painful reflection is that of a man at the end of his life, who regrets what he might have done, had he not been swept along so mercilessly by the stream of time.

A consuming longing overcomes the wretched solitary, lying before his cave; his desire is directed toward something indefinable, yet certain – "Todessehnsucht," a longing for release from time into the harmony of eternal peace.

On an enchanting summer night, when the landscape is transformed by the moonlight into an ethereal realm, the inhabitants of which direct their glances instinctively toward the heavens, a pair of lovers float down the river in a boat past the hermit's cave and their music fills the air and skies (p. 160) – "Aus dem Nachen wallte eine ätherische Musik in den Raum des Himmels empor." The concepts of night, music, and death are romantically synthesized; the longing for release from the roaring wheel of time is fulfilled for the mad hermit through the music of the lovers. The melody and harmony of music are the antitheses to the relentless rhythms of the time-wheel (or the complements of it); they are, as it were, the time-rhythms of eternity (p. 161) – "Mit dem ersten Tone der Musik und des Gesanges war dem nackten Heiligen das sausende Rad der Zeit verschwunden. Es waren die ersten Töne, die in diese Einöde fielen; die unbekannte Sehnsucht war gestillt, *der Zauber gelöst*, der verirrte Genius aus seiner irdischen Hülle befreit."

Wackenroder's hermit, therefore, figures in his obsession not only in an allegorical "Märchen" depicting the release of the individual from the crushing tempo of the time-wheel into the sphere of eternal harmony (music) and love, but, as "der verirrte Genius," in a kind of "Mythos." He becomes also the "Genius" of music released from the evil enchantment ("Zauber") of the maddening earthly rhythms. As "der verirrte Genius" he was condemned through his obsession to seek control of the terrible wheel; freed from this martyrdom, which characterized him alone, he is transformed into a kind of saint of heavenly "time" – music, arising, as it were, from the heart of love and resolving the cacophony of time into the rhythmic pattern of timeless harmony.

(3) While Wackenroder's "nackter Heilige" is possessed of a sacred madness, triumphing through music over his martyrdom at

the wheel of time, to be absorbed in mystic union with the harmony of the spheres, Hoffmann's *Serapion* is simply insane – one of many figures in whom the "poet of the unseen world" examines the peculiarities of the abnormal mind. In contrast to Wackenroder's hermit, however, Hoffmann's achieves supreme spiritual calm precisely because of his "Wahn."

The hermit, who believes that he is the martyred bishop-recluse, St. Serapion (we cannot say he "suffers" from a delusion, for he is utterly happy), takes up his solitary abode (like Schlemihl) on the site of the original hermitages in the Theban desert – in reality, a forest two hours from Bamberg. The original Serapion was, of course, one of these first Christian hermits; he was the Bishop of Thmuis near the upper Nile Delta (app. A. D. 350) and was driven by the Arian, Ptolemeus, from his seat – becoming a hermit in the Theban desert. The Serapion of Hoffmann's tale (there were eight by this name in church history – p. 7) was martyred in Alexandria under Emperor Ducius (p. 6).

The figure of Serapion in the "Novelle" is of interest, also, in connection with Hoffmann's circle of friends (Contessa, Hitzig, Koreff), "die Serapionsbrüder," which lent its name as title to the four volume collection of "Märchen" and "Novellen" (cf. Hewett-Thayer, *Hoffmann, Author of the Tales* – p. 102 ff.). The occasion of the first meeting of the "Bund" fell upon the fourteenth of November, Serapion's name-day in the church-calendar – the day, also, on which Hoffmann's mad hermit dies (p. 18). The hermit illustrates by his "Novellen," told to the narrator (p. 16), the poetic phantasy, which is heightened by his insanity, and which reveals his amazing capability to live and, thus, bring to life the creatures of his imagination – in a realistic manner, no matter how fantastic they may be. This conception of narrative embodied in the insane hermit provides the basis of Hoffmann's "serapiontisches Prinzip" of composition in the subsequent collections of tales.

The hermit, Serapion, had been the brilliant and poetically gifted son of a wealthy count, and had been distinguished by fiery imagination and deep insight into human existence (p. 4-5); he had also possessed a keen humor which made him widely popular and successful as a diplomat. Yet, for reasons which we do not discover (and which play no role, actually, in his hermithood), the young man suddenly vanished from the scene of his activity – to be found, subsequently, preaching in the mountain villages of the Tirol and dwelling in the wilds as a hermit (p. 5). All therapeutic attempts to remove his illusion resulted in violent fits of rage and madness on the part of the would-be holy man, whereupon the physician in the case found it most advisable to grant his patient's desire to lead the life of peace and freedom in the forest for which his subconsciousness so passionately longed (p. 6).

With profound understanding and sympathy (we dare say, with admiration) for the abnormal mental state, Hoffmann sets before us, paradoxically, the healthiest example of a hermit to be encountered in this part of the study – and he is a madman. In his hermithood, he is completely in harmony with God, nature, and the world, and, but for his illusion, one would take him for a mentally sound, intelligent human being (p. 6).

Serapion's reputation among the peasants in the area reveals the fact that his life is, in a sense, a fruitful one; his influence upon those with whom he comes into contact is healthy and beneficial and he enjoys the respect of the country folk (p. 4) – "Die Leute sagen, er sei nicht richtig im Kopfe, aber er ist ein lieber frommer Herr, der niemandem etwas zuleide tut und der uns im Dorfe mit andächtigen Reden recht erbaut und uns guten Rat erteilt, wie er nur kann." As a hermit, Serapion is no shy fugitive from the world, but rather a vigorous man of the out-doors who seeks peace and harmony in God through a life devoted to natural living and piety. He has built his own hut, made its rough furniture, and planted a garden of vegetables and flowers around it (p. 6). Except when he is engaged in conversing with men of his own philosophical cloth such as Ambrosius of Kamaldoli (p. 4), Ariosto, Dante, Petrarch, or the church-teacher, Evagrius (p. 14), Serapion is more than happy to receive visitors – "Ohne im mindesten von jener Frömmigkeit abzuweichen, die dem ziemt, der sein ganzes Leben Gott und der Kirche geweiht, ist mir jener asketische Cynismus fremd, in den viele von meinen Brüdern verfielen und dadurch statt der gerühmten Stärke innere Ohnmacht, ja offenbare Zerrüttung aller Geisteskräfte bewiesen."

The impression made upon the narrator by Serapion is, as we have said, that of a healthy, energetic man at one with the world of nature (and men) about him. As Hoffmann approaches the hermitage on his second visit (p. 7), he finds his recluse busy in his garden with hoe and spade. His harmony in nature is indicated by his intimacy with the doves and deer of his forest abode – which he feeds while singing a pious song – "So schien er mit den Tieren des Waldes in vollkommner Eintracht zu leben. Keine Spur des Wahnsinns war in seinem Gesicht zu finden, dessen milde Züge von seltener Ruhe und Heiterkeit zeugten." Although he prefers to avoid company in the evening, he enjoys receiving visitors earlier in the day, especially on pleasant mornings. Serapion's madness is of that sort to which Hoffmann is inclined to attribute particular mental acuteness and energy – this is illustrated not only by the mastery of the hermit as a "Novellist," whose marvelous phantasy is distinguished by the ability to experience, which makes the irrational a reality ("serapiontisches Prinzip"), but also by the astuteness and logic with which he opposes Hoffmann's attempt to dislodge his fixed idea. Hoffmann likes to use madness ironically as a description of genius, (cf. also *Rat Krespel, Ritter Gluck*). With systematic patience (and not a little sarcasm), the hermit refutes every single point made by the visitor, who had digested a number of authoritative works on the nature of such cases; and the opening words of the madman are such that they confuse the feelings of Hoffmann from the outset – (p. 11) "Bin ich nun wirklich wahnsinnig, so kann nur ein Verrückter wähnen, dass er imstande sein werde, mir die fixe Idee, die der Wahnsinn erzeugt hat, auszureden. Wäre dies möglich, so gäb' es bald keinen Wahnsinnigen mehr auf der ganzen Erde, denn der Mensch könnte gebieten über die geistige Kraft, die nicht sein Eigentum, sondern nur anvertrautes Gut der höhern Macht ist, die darüber waltet."

The point which Serapion actually does make is that it matters not a whit whether he is a madman or not; what is important is that he lives, to his mind, an ideal life. (He passes beautifully over the martyrdom by drawing and quartering; he feels now and then only a piercing headache and pulling in his limbs, which remind him of the torture endured (p. 9) – God had thrown the blessed veil of forgetfulness over these details.) He considers his calm of spirit in hermithood to be a blessing from above and from his point of view (or the reader's), it is, indeed, that. Consequently, we may formulate Serapion's condition as a bizarre kind of sacred gift; he wishes his visitor the same blessing as that which has been granted to him (p. 14) – "Möge dich, o mein Bruder! der Himmel schon auf Erden, die Ruhe, die Heiterkeit geniessen lassen, die mich erquickt und stärkt. Fürchte nicht die Schauer der tiefen Einsamkeit, nur in ihr geht dem frommen Gemüt solch ein Leben auf!"

Hoffmann's Serapion is a model hermit; he dwells in peace and harmony with nature and in benevolence toward the world and men. Neither is his spirit troubled by torments from the past, nor is the tranquillity of his ideal and stimulating hermithood ever disturbed by the interference of antipathetic forces (except in the case of the narrator). Could such complete peace and harmony be realized in isolation? Though Serapion's hermithood is a unique one, we cannot base a conclusion on any attitude of the author; such a question clearly does not concern him. We may offer only an enigmatic answer – Serapion is insane and his hermithood is phantasy projected, as it were, into reality. He stands apart, therefore, from all hermits of this part of our study – apart even from those in whose development toward solitude madness plays a role.

In this chapter we have concentrated upon subjective problems in hermithood. Without over-simplifying our composite character analysis, we may divide those hermits whose background involves an infortunate love, as well as the others, into two groups – those who find peace in solitude and those who do not.

In the first category, we place, for example, the old hermit of *Erwin and Elmire*, whose spirit after death becomes equated with the tranquillity and healing power of nature, then, Balduin (*Walter*), who finds in nature the original purity and innocence which is vitiated by forces in the outer world, and finally, Lenz's "Waldbruder", Werdo Senne, and Serapion – all, as we have seen, radically different, but dwelling in ideal reality in nature. Erwin, himself, in Goethe's operetta, Walter, and Wackenroder's "Nackter Heiliger" are, on the other hand, not able to attain spiritual calm.

Certain figures in this chapter may also be considered from another point of view – those who find a new and compatible reality in the solitary life. Among these, of course, are Herz, Werdo Senne, Lenau's morbid hermit reliving the past, and Serapion. The sense of a new, deeper, more kindred reality, the world recreated in isolation from within, is the most positive aspect of hermithood and the goal of this way of life – Serapion is an extreme embodiment of the latter theme, and, as such, is transitional to the fourth and final part of our study.

In this chapter we have examined, through the analysis of subjective problems and motifs, the struggle in isolation to achieve peace of mind. In so far as the hermit attains such tranquillity, he does it through re-evaluation of reality in terms of the world of nature (re-creating the world from within). In the analysis of subjective problems, the hermit appears at his "loneliest" in conflict with those forces out of which his problem grew and which retain a grasp upon his spirit.

In the following chapter, we take the last step in our study; now the hermit appears in relationship to that world for which he has rejected society and which offers, potentially, the desired harmony of spirit and nature where he stands upon the invisible border between this life and the next.

CHAPTER IV

THE HERMIT AND NATURE

In nature, the hermit hopes to find the ultimate, universal values in life, for which he has rejected those of society (II), and in this realm he seeks to attain spiritual calm and healing for a soul wounded by unhappy developments in the past – nature is a refuge from hostile forces in the world, and transforms tragic experience into a new reality (III). In this final portion, we shall examine the hermit in his relationship to nature, which becomes for him the final sphere of his development in this life – a revelation of the eternal spirit, to which he is reunited. We have seen (for example, in *Godwi* and in Wackenroder's *Märchen*) that the emotion of indefinable longing, most specifically the longing toward nature, is essentially "Todessehnsucht" – a longing for reunion with the elements of eternity. All "Todessehnsucht" is, especially in works of Romanticism, an unearthly and profound longing for such reunification.

(1) The figure of the hermit, Alfonso, in Wieland's *Oberon* illustrates many of the important characteristics associated with the solitaries of subsequent romantic works – for Wieland is, in significant respects, a forerunner of Romanticism. Like Eichendorff's Don Diego, the recluse in *Oberon* is a former Spanish knight who finds his earthly paradise on a remote tropical island and, like Novalis' Hohenzollern, the death of his wife and sons had, in part, motivated his hermithood (the circumstances of shipwreck are also similar to those in Chamisso's *Salas y Gomez*, the hero of which, however, is not a hermit). Alfonso (and most subsequent romantic hermits) is an aged man and, as such, personifies spiritual intimacy with nature, preparing for his impending union with it in death. It is interesting to note that several lines referring to the shipwreck also suggest the sea as a source of eternal life surrounding his adopted world, the island (VIII, 16) "bevor er aus den Wogen/Der Welt geborgen ward–". This is comparable to the visions of gleaming endless waters symbolizing eternity in Kerner's *Die Heimatlosen*. Waldvater had been a seaman and Serpentin had these visions, while, in the "Märchen" of Sililie, Goldener departs across such an infinite sea. The conception of the sea as an isolating medium (insulate and isolate are variations of a common stem) and of the island-motif connect the hermit-theme to that of the island-paradise in the

"Robinsonaden." There is some "internal" evidence that Wieland's picture was influenced by the Robinson Crusoe motif (e.g. the "two-faced" island, with one barren and one verdant portion).

As we have briefly mentioned, Alfonso has a background which might be termed traditional for the hermit (Trevrizent, Simplicissimus, Balduin, Count Robert, Hohenzollern, Don Diego, Paul, in Uhland's *König Eginhard* – all had sought solitude after a life of varied and rich activity, usually spent in knighthood or a courtly or military career). He had experienced a luxurious and active past as knight and courtier. Like many of our hermits, he, too, had come to consider the empty splendor of wordly ways a vain thing. He had been reared in royal service, and had competed with countless others for glory and recognition (VIII., 16) –

"Dem schimmernden Gespenst, das ewige Opfer heischet
Und, gleich dem Stein der Narrn, die Hoffnung ewig täuschet."

Having evaluated this life as illusory and barren of all deeper validity, he felt the shipwreck to be a bizarre stroke of fortune, which released him from the burdens of courtly existence (as did Balduin's losses by fire), and spared himself, his wife, and his friend to pass their remaining years in isolation (VIII., 17).

The successive deaths of his three sons, his wife, and his best friend, however, turned Alfonso's thoughts toward the grave, and the world, itself, seemed to be a very tomb. To excape the silent reminder of his sorrow, he fled with a servant to the rocky isle which became the scene of his final hermithood.

Once every tie with the world is broken and the deaths of his loved ones have reoriented his entire being, Alfonso's senses are opened and made receptive to the elements of nature and, through them, his spirit achieves awareness of its eternal relationship with all about him; a profound contentment comes over him and he finds a new life – (VIII., 22)

"–die Nüchternheit, die Stille,
Die reine freie Luft durchläuterten sein Blut,
Entwölkten seinen Sinn, belebten seinen Mut.
Er spürte nun, dass aus der ewigen Fülle
Des Lebens Balsam auch für seine Wunden quille."

Nature is conceived (not only in the personification of its forces in the fairy rulers, Oberon and Titania) as the positive medium through which the divine spirit reaches out to soothe and heal the soul of man.

Thus, Alfonso's abode, shut off from the rest of the island by the bleak cliffs and dense forest, suggests the pulsating heart of nature, itself. Its eternal characteristics are indicated further by the green earth and rich foliage, which, even in autumn, are protected from the blighting northwind – it is another world, an enchanting fairyland where figs and oranges still bloom, although their season is past (VIII., 12). The remoteness of this "Elysium" from the outer world implies, also, a nearness to the pervading spirit of nature – Titania, its elfin queen and genius, had created the secluded paradise as a refuge for herself, until she might be reconciled with Oberon (VIII., 65-66). The marvelous glade, then, assumes a supernatural, ethereal quality through her presence. It breathes a vital healing power, and becomes for the hermit the medium of his metaphysical affinity with eternal life – Alfonso's intimate relationship with nature is the basis of his rapport with the spiritual beyond and, accordingly, his hermitage symbolizes the final stage and attenuation of his physical life.

As we have already inferred, the death of those closest to him had made him acutely sensitive to the world of the spirit; through its intermediary realm, nature, it applies its healing power – nature is the very revelation of the transcendental. Left utterly alone after the passing of his loyal servant, the hermit's essential spiritualization ("Vergeistigung") becomes an accomplished state through his heightened receptivity to the impulses about him, through nature he reaches toward his loved ones beyond (VIII., 26) –

> "–Doch desto fester kehrte
> Sein stiller Geist nun ganz nach jener Welt sich hin,
> Der, was er einst geliebt, itzt alles angehörte,
> Der auch er selbst schon mehr als dieser angehörte!"

Yet, the specific longing for the dead is transformed (as in the case of Werdo Senne) into a suprarational, harmonious intimacy with the ethereal – natural realm of his environment, and the process of the transformation is a recreation of the world from within (VIII., 27)

> "Ihm wird, als fühl' er dann die dünne Scheidwand fallen,
> Die ihn noch kaum von seinen Lieben trennt;
> Sein Innres schliesst sich auf, die heil'ge Flamme brennt,
> Aus seiner Brust empor; sein Geist, im reinen Lichte
> Der unsichtbaren Welt, sieht himmlische Gesichte."

At night (to Wieland, as to the Romanticists, a realm of "Unendlichkeit" and other-worldliness) – (VIII., 26)

> "wenn vor dem äussern Sinn
> Wie in ihr erstes Nichts die Körper sich verlieren –"

Alfonso feels a phantom touch upon his cheek and, in half-slumber, he is aware of the echoes of angelic voices from the grove outside his hut. Yet this consciousness of most intimate communion with the universal forces does not leave the hermit during daylight hours of activity, for the experience had awakened completely and forever in his innermost being (VIII., 29) the purest of all senses (which the poet refuses to name, preferring, rather, to remain silent on the edge of the abyss, as he says). Undoubtedly, "der reinste aller Sinne" is essentially "Todessehnsucht," equated, here, (as in Hölderlin, Novalis and Kerner) with the emotion of harmony of the entire being with all elements (a conception related, also, to the "Fühlbarkeit" of Werther, to which we alluded in connection with Blasius in chapter II). It represents for Wieland the inutterable, for it is a conscious insight into the Absolute beyond the thin "dividing wall" (VIII., 27). The partition between this life and the next has fallen before the hermit's inner eye, since his intimate communion with nature in solitude has granted him a means of penetrating it – a means accessible to the recluse alone – (VIII., 29) –

"So fliesst zuletzt unmerklich Erd' und Himmel
In seinem Geist in Eins."

This sense of suprarational recognition gained through such a communion distinguishes the hermit from other men; although he is a secular recluse, Alfonso is endowed with a natural-spiritual power – he becomes a kind of priest of nature. Indeed, suggestions of his identification with the pervading spirit are apparent from Amanda's (Rezia's) initial impression of him. She falls upon her knees before him as before the genius of the sacred, seemingly enchanted glade in which he dwells (VIII., 13). To both Amanda and Hüon, whom Alfonso receives into his hermitage, he often appears to be a protective spirit ("Schutzgeist"), perhaps Oberon, himself, in the guise of a hermit to do penance for their guilt (VIII., 33).

In the capacity of confessor, the worthy Alfonso urges Hüon to disclose the source of his misery, offering to do penance for him (similar to the theme of vicarious atonement in Trevrizent), to open to him the gates of redemption (VIII., 6). In the same capacity, he hears the tale of Hüon's adventures and the guilt which Amanda and her knight had incurred through breach of trust with Oberon, nature's royal elf (VIII, 35-37). Since the lovers had offended Oberon and, through him, as it were, his realm, abstinence and the purifying effect of the simple hardy life in nature combine as fitting atonements – thus, too, a strengthening for the ordeal of faith and loyalty which they are to endure at the court of Almansor in Tunis (X-XII). As the dedicated spokesman of nature, Alfonso is the ideal mentor of the young couple in their penance and initiation into the cleansing life of his sacred hermitage. The hermit, therefore, becomes, as we have said, a secular priest and interpreter of the element through which the "Weltseele" reaches the soul of man. He performs, in this respect, what might be called an educational function for the protagonists of the epic, Hüon and Rezia, at a crucial stage of their development (as does Trevrizent for Parzifal, Hohenzollern for Heinrich von Ofterdingen, and, to an extent, Don Diego for Antonio).

We have referred previously to implications of the hermit's identification with the genius of the secluded paradise; we have also indicated the essentially symbolic and spiritual character of his dwelling place – a quality derived specifically from the presence of Titania (cf. VIII., 66) – and we have traced the stages of his spiritualization ("Vergeistigung") through the increased receptivity to the natural forces. While the suggestions of his identification with the pervading spirit of the hermitage cannot, of course, be taken at surface value (for Titania, the personification of this spirit, dwells there too), they do point toward his ultimate union with it in death – the final stage of his spiritualization.

The angelic voices which Alfonso had heard during the night (cf. VIII., 27) were those of Titania and her attendant Sylphs (VIII., 66) and it was the elfin Queen, herself, whose passing seemed a phantom brushing on his cheek – this fanciful connection of the hermit's sensitivity to the impulses from nature with its personification in Titania lends a definite, we might almost say concrete, quality to the implication of his eventual reunion with the pervading spirit in death. A further word with respect to a possible symbolic connotation of Titania's grotto may add weight indirectly to our conception of her as the genius of the natural spirit and of the death of the hermit as complete reunification with it. The entrance to the grotto is impassable; it is as if an invisible gate barred all who would from entering – Hüon and Alfonso tempted by its iridescent beauty in the morning sun had often wished to go in, but had felt an unusual resistance – "ein wunderbares Grauen" (VIII., 71). The invisible obstacle at the entrance to Titania's cave may well be considered the ultimate equivalent of the thin "Scheidwand" (VIII., 27) which had fallen from before the hermit's soul in his new-found intimacy with the universal (nature) spirit (in preparation for his eventual and final "Vergeistigung"). The curious sense of horror ("Grauen") felt at the brink of this portal is like that expressed by the poet when he refuses to name "the purest of all senses" (VIII., 29) – it is the involuntary awe of confrontation with the Absolute which one cannot comprehend in this life (an emotion similar to, though less violent than that which turns Faust's face from tne Earth-Spirit). Only Amanda (Rezia) is able to pass through the magic portal; that is possible because she is to give birth to her child in the sacred precinct of the grotto (VIII., 75) – it is the heart and soul of nature from which life emerges and into which, in death, it is finally taken.

Alfonso's life has its "diesseitig" aspects, however, for it is he who instructs Hüon in the cultivation of the garden and in constructing shelter and hearth for Amanda (VIII., 40-41) –

> "'Nichts unterhält so gut'" versichert ihn der Greis,
> 'Die Sinne mit der Pflicht in Frieden,
> Als fleissig sie durch Arbeit zu ermüden;
> Nichts bringt sie leichter aus dem Gleis
> Als müss'ge Träumerei'."

Through the activity suggested by the recluse, Hüon finds a means of maintaining his oath of abstinence. For Alfonso (as for Novalis' hermit and Eichendorff's), hermithood is a way of life incompatible to the young, to whom isolation is highly unnatural and in whose veins the strength for deeds yet unaccomplished still pulses. Although wordly existence has no further significance for Alfonso, he sympathizes with the young people, reading the unfulfilled hopes in their souls and in the tears, which they vainly attempt to conceal – (IX., 27)

> "tadelt nicht die unfreiwilligen Triebe
> Und frischt sie nur, so lang' als ihren Lauf
> Das Schicksal hemmt, zu stillem Hoffen auf."

Yet, the hermit's entire being is, as we have seen, directed toward its final absorption into the cosmos; his earthly life has become a dream and his mind dwells upon the flight of his soul into the true existence (IX, 29) –

> "es war, als wehe schon
> Ein Hauch von Himmelsluft zu ihm herüber
> Und trag' ihn sanft empor, indem es sprach."

The more sensitive feminine instinct of Amanda is somehow aware that the pious man's final stage of withdrawal from life is at hand (IX, 29) – she had been in the sacred grotto to bear her child. Alfonso feels it too –

> "'Mir', fuhr er fort, 'mir reichèn sie die Hände
> Vom Ufer jenseits schon, mein Lauf ist bald zu Ende' –"

and upon the threshold of his "Vergeistigung" he foretells the hardships which await the young people – joys and trials alternate through life (pleasures are a strengthening for subsequent pains). The wordly vicissitude and bliss become dreams and nothing accompanies the soul to its goal (IX, 31) –

> "Nichts als der gute Schatz, den ihr in euer Herz
> Gesammelt, Wahrheit, Lieb' und innerlicher Frieden,
> Und die Erinnerung, dass weder Lust noch Schmerz
> Euch je vom treuen Hang an eure Pflicht geschieden."

At the close of the evening on which the hermit expresses the sum of his life experience, he embraces Hüon and Amanda in a last farewell, and enters his hut with tear-filled eyes. In the past, his soul at rest had heard the ethereal voices from the enchanted grove, but on this night Titania, in fearful anticipation of Amanda's future peril, flies forth from her dwelling place, taking with her the baby for safekeeping (IX., 32). In this very night, too, Alfonso's sublimation is completed; he is discovered dead on the following morning. The departure of Titania coincides with the hermit's death; his soul has passed through the sacred portal, as it were, and has become one with the universal spirit of nature. The hermit's "Naturvergeistigung" is implied not only by Titania's flight from the garden paradise, simultaneous with the hermit's decease, but also by the fact that the "Elysium" surrounding the hermitage has been transformed (IX., 44). The plants and garden have withered, the forest is blighted, and the entire glade becomes as bleak as the rest of the island. The departure of the genius, with which the hermit's soul in death is identified, robs the hermitage of its aspect of eternal life.

The hermithood of Alfonso, then, represents the most remote station of life, one attained only after a wealth of experience and suffering and in advanced age, when the innermost being has been directed toward the realm beyond; hermithood is that phase in which the final stages of spiritualization through nature take place and in which the soul of the hermit is ultimately reunited with the pervading spirit. Nature becomes the realm through which the individual attains to the cosmic harmony. Thus, Alfonso's relationship to nature provides a kind of preview, essentially, of the hermit's position in Romanticism. We may cite a thought of Schelling, the most representative of romantic philosophers (cf. also W. Silz, *Early German Romanticism* – p. 8), which calls to mind our interpretation of Alfonso's "Vergeistigung" and reunification with the spirit of nature in death. In his *Ideen zu einer Philosophie der Natur* (Werke, Bd. I, p. 158-159), he says of "das Absolute," which is embodied in nature, "– da nun sein Wesen ein Produzieren ist und es die Form nur aus sich selbst nehmen kann, es selbst aber reine Identität ist, so muss auch die Form *diese Identität*, und also Wesen und Form in ihm *eines und dasselbe*, nämlich die gleiche reine Absolutheit sein." The hermit here attains at last that "absolute Identität des Geistes in uns und der Natur ausser uns" of which Schelling speaks.

We have seen, too, that Wieland's hermit is a secular one; his spiritual realm is in nature. This is true of a majority of hermits in the present chapter, and most particularly of those belonging to Romanticism. The hermit in Oberon is a forerunner of the solitaries embodying the romantic "Naturfrömmigkeit" which takes the place of more orthodox Christian concepts of the cosmos. Thus, the hermit figure becomes a striking exponent of the interpretation of life through nature (cf. also Korff, *Geist der Goethezeit*, Bd. IV, p. 372-374).

(2) The hero of Hölderlin's *Hyperion* is consciously dedicated to a religion of nature, a natural piety (cf. also Korff, *Geist der Goethezeit*, IV, p. 375 ff), in which he sees the only hope of a rejuvenated humanity. Hyperion's development to hermithood is the history (more properly, elegy) of his successive disappointments with the race of men as he has come to know it and, at the same time, of his attainment to complete harmony in nature. In proportion as he experiences disillusionment with the state of the world, his sensitivity to the divine aspect of nature is intensified by his suffering ("Leiden"), and brings him to the conviction that solitude devoted to the nature-spirit is his inevitable lot. The specific experiences with Alabanda and in the war of liberation against the Turks, as well as the observations of humanity, form the bases of Hyperion's disillusionment and dejection, while, opposed to these, the Adamas and Diotoma "Erlebnisse," together with his inherent understanding of the divine elements about him, contribute to his rejection of a vain world in favor of solitary communion with nature.

The form of the work, consisting as it does of Hyperion's letters written in hermithood, permits the retrospective evaluation of experience in terms of the hermit's state of mind at the time of writing; this presentation, in addition to the essentially lyrical expression, lends to the whole its elegiac character, revealing the past transfigured through the shimmering veil of memory – from the point of view of the hermit the past is bathed in the ethereal light of the spirit with which he communes.

Hyperion's disillusionment with his age derives from the degeneration of men; his contemporaries have broken the bond of naive understanding with nature, which once rendered them complete and harmonious – reflection, pedantry, dry speculation have torn humanity up by the roots (as we shall see, the plant is a profound image of the godly relationship between nature and man). The jackal's howling amid the ruins of Greek antiquity implies the corruption and destruction of earlier sacred concord through the perverse development of humanity (p. 5). This degeneration is, for Hyperion, universal, for he is ashamed and disappointed not only of his modern Greek countrymen (p. 6) but of the Germans, too, from whom (as the revivers of classic idealism) he had expected, at the least, consolation; instead, they had revealed to him a duality and discord exaggerated by their specialization in industry, science, and religion (p. 201). His own fatherland is a garden of the dead, in which the hermit dwells, seeking to steep himself in the aspect which recalls the innocence and completeness of his childhood (p. 9) – that he may recover the sense of communion with the divinity of nature, the sense of harmony destroyed by activity and experience in the world. The temptation to engage in violent activity (such as the war against the Turks) foreign to his nature had played a major role in Hyperion's disillusionment and consequent suffering, for this drive had been based upon love for the world, the essence of the nature-spirit, and upon the desire to rejuvenate humanity through his own idealism – (p. 6) "O hätt' ich doch nie gehandelt! Um wie manche Hoffnung wär ich reicher.'"

It would, of course, be quite inaccurate to call *Hyperion* a "Rahmenerzählung" in letter form, but the faint suggestion of such a form is, nevertheless, present. The initial letters of the novel concentrate upon the hero's state of mind in hermithood and his conception of nature as religion, while the concluding letters reveal again the communion of the hermit with nature in the light of the parallel streams of experience which lie between – the experiences of disillusionment and those which lead him once more to the heart of nature.

Hyperion's most intense desire is the instinctive urge to surrender his entire being to nature, to let himself be absorbed into its divine ether and to absorb, in turn, its eternal spirit, as do the plants and blossoms of the field (p. 7) – "und mir ist, als öffnet' ein verwandter Geist mir die Arme, als löste der Schmerz der Einsamkeit sich auf ins Leben der Gottheit." This emotion is not religiosity, but, rather, religion, itself. To be one with all that lives, to return in blessed forgetfulness of self into the cosmos, would be the ecstatic fulfillment of his inherent potentialities – such a communion with nature is the true heaven (p. 7). In this union the concept of death has no meaning; eternal youth is its essence – a blessing which would rejuvenate mankind.

In the child, alone, such a state exists to the fullest extent. Hyperion recalls with longing the innocence of his own childhood spent in instinctive consonance with the all – (p. 9) "Es (das Kind) ist ganz was es ist, und darum ist es so schön." In its original circumstances, the child is characterized by freedom, peace, and beauty; yet, in adulthood, it is fated to be robbed of its innocence and effortless happiness by the perverse influences of men (p. 10). The Romantic estimation of childhood is connected here with the philosophy of hermithood as an attempt to return to a state of uncomplicated simplicity and innocence (this conception of childhood is akin also to that of English Romanticism – cf. Wordsworth, *Ode on Intimations of Immortality*). The ideal state of childhood is like that of the tender plant, rooted in the earth, and blossoming to eternal light – drawing its life and nourishment, not only from the soil, but from the spirit-ether into which it extends. This image of the plant recurs like a leit-motif throughout the work, always to suggest the full relationship to nature.) The idealization of childhood is reminiscent of that which is standard in New Testament Christianity, but, it is to be remembered, such an idealization for the hermit, Hyperion, is an embodiment of his "Naturreligion". Hyperion conclusively identifies God with earth, His creation, (p. 11) – "O wenn sie eines Vaters Tochter ist, die herrliche Natur, ist das Herz der Tochter nicht sein Herz? Ihr Innerstes, ists nicht Er?"

Adamas' teaching stimulates this "Naturglaube" in the young Hyperion, for the wise mentor lives in the utmost intimacy with nature, and exemplifies deep understanding of it to his pupil. Yet, Adamas feels a strong impulse to better humanity, to remold it to his ideal and, not having found men capable of this ennoblement (p. 12-14), he comes to Greece in the hope of discovering the genius of that model race. In Hyperion, he finds his protegé (p. 14) – "Wie vor einer Pflanze, wenn ihr Friede den strebenden Geist besänftigt, und die einfältige Genügsamkeit wiederkehrt in die Seele – so stand er vor mir." Adamas recognizes in Hyperion the naive understanding of nature, the integration of his being with it – he stands before the boy as if the latter were a "plant."– Together teacher and pupil wander over the eternal landscape, drinking in its spirit and discovering the reliques of pristine greatness (p. 15-16) – "edle Einfalt und stille Grösse." Thus, Adamas reveals the character of ancient Greece to Hyperion as an ideal to be recreated in the Greeks of his own age and he foresees the young man's destiny, exhorting him to be like his namesake, the sun-god – to become a prophet of that spirit-light of nature which had illumined his forefathers (p. 17). Adamas, however, recognizes the pain and frustration which inevitably await the idealistic youth; he prophesies Hyperion's eventual hermithood (p. 18) – "Du wirst einsam sein, mein Liebling! – du wirst sein wie der Kranich, den seine Brüder zurückliessen in rauher Jahrzeit, indes sie den Frühling suchen im fernen Lande." The desire to bring about among his contemporaries a renaissance of the natural harmony and "Naturfrömmigkeit" envisioned in antiquity is doomed to end in the disillusionment and suffering which is, in part, Hyperion's fate and which plays an important role in his turn to isolation. It is Hyperion's destiny to suffer, as we have already indicated, because the motivating force of nature in him is love (p. 18) – "Das macht uns arm bei allem Reichtum, dass wir nicht allein sein können, dass die Liebe in uns, solange wir leben, nicht erstirbt." It is love which binds Hyperion to his "Schicksal," but is love, too, which leads him ultimately to tranquillity and concord in nature (an elegiac tranquillity, to be sure).

The departure of Adamas for Asia in search of a race of unique excellence leaves Hyperion alone with the hope of redeeming his contemporaries burning in his heart; he also inherits from Adamas the urge to seek out the embodiment of his ideal – to find a kindred soul, in whose companionship he may strengthen his own conviction and purpose (p. 27) – "Die Unheilbarkeit des Jahrhunderts war mir aus so manchem, was ich erzähle und nicht erzähle, sichtbar geworden, und der schöne Trost, in *einer* Seele meine Welt zu finden, mein Geschlecht in einem freundlichen Bilde zu umarmen, auch der gebrach mir."

Adamas' revelation of ancient Greece fires the impulse in the younger man to revive its spirit in his own time; the Adamas "Erlebnis," consequently, prepares directly for the association with Alabanda, as well as for the disappointment and disillusionment which result from it.

In Alabanda, Hyperion sees the heroic "Ganzheit" of the great past personified (p. 29) – "Wie ein junger Titan, schritt der herrliche Fremdling unter dem Zwergengeschlechte daher, das mit freudiger Scheue an seiner Schöne sich weidete, seine Höhe mass und seine Stärke." Although his friend is the man of noble aspiration and action, he lacks the divine inspiration of nature; the state is his ideal and the destruction of all that is decadent in it (p. 35) – "die Mine bereite mir einer, dass ich die trägen Klötze aus der Erde sprenge!" Destruction, however, plays no role in the enthusiasm of the nature-apostle – "Wo möglich, lehnt man sanft sie (Klötze) auf die Seite." For Hyperion the state is only the wall protecting the blossoming fruit of humanity; not through force or the supremacy of the state, but rather through the advent of the new faith ("Naturfrömmigkeit"), will humanity be raised from its decadence (p. 40) – "Dann, wann die Lieblingin der Zeit, die jüngste schönste Tochter der Zeit, die neue Kirche hervorgehn wird –, wann das erwachte Gefühl des Göttlichen dem Menschen seine Gottheit und seiner Brust die schöne Jugend bringen wird –." Alabanda, nevertheless, joins the band of nihilists to rout out and eliminate forcibly the decay in the state, and Hyperion is left destitute and disillusioned. His faith, alone, consoles him and he sees in the alternating aspirations and adversities of his life the revelation of his godhead, nature (p. 48) – "Bestehet ja das Leben der Welt in Wechsel des Entfaltens und Entschliessens, in Ausflug und in Rückkehr zu sich selbst, warum nicht auch das Herz des Menschen?" The conception of the human heart, its "excursions" and its return into itself, is clearly a suggestion of Hyperions's eventual hermithood as an end process comparable to that of nature, where all returns through the course of existence to itself – eventually, hermithood, for Hyperion, of course, illustrates the "homecoming" of the spirit of nature in the individual to itself (as in the harmony of childhood) (cf. also p. 7).

The experience in the war for Greek independence, in which Hyperion is reconciled to Alabanda, produces in him the ultimate disappointment in his countrymen, and causes him to give up all hope of a renaissance in his own time. Filled with the loftiest aspiration, Hyperion leads his men against Misitra – (p. 150) "Diotima, ich möchte dieses werdende Glück nicht um die schönste Lebenszeit des alten Griechenlands vertauschen–." When the city has been taken, however, his comrades show their bestiality, their unworthiness of his high hopes for them; they plunder, rob, and murder countryman and enemy alike, revealing their cowardice in flight before a far weaker force of Albanians (p. 152-154). Hyperion is banished and cursed as a common thief and rebel (p. 155). He is, himself, crushed by the fiasco and forced to admit failure (p. 153) "Diese trauernde Erde! die nackte! so ich kleiden wollte mit heiligen Hainen, so ich schmücken wollte mit allen Blumen des griechischen Lebens!" Although Hyperion attempts to throw away his life in a subsequent naval battle, he survives miraculously the hand-to-hand combat and the inferno of the flaming ship (p. 162) – "und das Schicksal schien mich zu achten in meiner Verzweiflung." Yet, it is the healing power of nature and his faith in it which gives Hyperion back to life, albeit resigned by disillusionment to the surrender of his ambition (p. 164) – "O heilige Pflanzenwelt! – wir streben und sinnen, und haben doch dich! wir ringen mit sterblichen Kräften Schönes zu baun, und es wächst doch sorglos neben uns auf."

The strengthening conviction of the divinity of nature which Hyperion carries with him into the war and which revives him after his dismal failure are largely inspired by the experience with Diotima. In her, he finds the complete harmony which he had longed to behold in a human soul (p. 68) – "Ich hab es einmal gesehen, das Einzige, das meine Seele suchte, und die Vollendung, die wir über die Sterne hinauf entfernen, die wir hinausschieben bis ans Ende der Zeit, die hab' ich gegenwärtig gefühlt." She is beauty personified (p. 68); she symbolizes that concept of "Schönheit" which for Hyperion implies the perfect, instinctive union of the individual soul with the pervading spirit. It is this ideal, embodied in Diotima, which accompanies him into hermithood and irradiates it.

In her infinite "child-like" concord, Diotima is a revelation of the sacred; she is nature (p. 71) – "Diotimas Auge öffnete sich weit, und leise, wie eine Knospe sich aufschliesst, schloss das liebe Gesichtchen vor den Lüften des Himmels sich auf, ward lauter Sprache und

Seele, und, als begänne sie den Flug in die Wolken, stand sanft emporgestreckt die ganze Gestalt, in leichter Majestät, und berührte kaum mit den Füssen die Erde." (Here, too, the opening bud simile suggests the perfect state of communion.) Her heart is at home among the flowers as if it were one of them (p. 73). The world of nature to her is a household in which all souls are eternal members (p. 74) – a belief which paraphrases Hyperion's faith in the return of the heart (soul) into itself in the course of life (cf. p. 48). Hyperion's hermithood becomes, in this light, an "actus fidet" and in solitude, the hermit communes with her and nature at once – for through her death, she becomes imperishably one with its spirit.

We have seen in our discussion of Hyperion's relationship with Adamas that the older man had dedicated his pupil to a higher existence and, at the same time, that he had prophesied the loneliness which would be the lot of the sun-god's namesake among men. We have also observed that a miraculous chance had preserved Hyperion's life in battle. With Diotima, too, Hyperion had relived the glory of ancient Athens (p. 112-113) – "Die Natur war Priesterin und der Mensch ihr Gott" – and she had pointed out his destiny prior to his departure for war (p. 119) – "Du wirst Erzieher unsers Volks." This would have been his natural mission, but his recourse to violence (war) vitiated it.

The disaster of the war and the terrible disillusionment for both Hyperion and Diotima is largely responsible for her death. Another factor is her realization that his love for her does not suffice to fill his life, that his masculine ambition and thirst for action will take him out of her life forever. She unselfishly encourages him, however, to fulfill himself – while she derives consolation from her belief in their eventual spiritual reunion in the eternal divinity of nature (from which nothing can be lost and in which all things return – see conclusion of this discussion). The idealism which she had felt in exhorting Hyperion to educate the Greeks withers and their future together is made impossible. Diotima insists upon separation, for she will bring forth no children in a world of slavery and degenerated values (p. 171) – "die armen Pflanzen welkten mir ja doch in dieser Dürre vor den Augen weg." In the realization of Hyperion's imperishable love for humanity and of the pain and disappointment which would await him in further attempts to revive his race, she urges him to turn from men, to devote himself to the eternal divinity in nature – to become a hermit (p. 171) – "du kehrest zu den Göttern, kehrst ins heilige freie, jugendliche Leben der Natur, wovon du ausgingst, und das ist ja dein Verlangen nur und auch das meine."– No ordinary reunion proves possible for the lovers but through such solitary communion on the part of Hyperion. In her final letter to him (p. 194), Diotima passionately voices once more her belief in immortality and union with nature – "Wir trennen uns nur, um inniger einig zu sein, göttlicher-friedlich mit allem, mit uns. Wir sterben, um zu leben."

The trip to Germany, which Diotima had suggested (p. 118) as a means of seeking greatness and beauty among a presumably more fortunate people, is a wretched failure; Hyperion finds there nothing worthy of the name, "Mensch" – (p. 206) "Und wehe dem Fremdling, der aus Liebe wandert, und zu solchem Volke kommt, und dreifach wehe dem, der, so wie ich, von grossem Schmerz getrieben, ein Bettler meiner Art, zu solchem Volke kommt!" There he finds no love of beauty, no honoring of genius in the artist, but only slavishness; completely defeated in his desire to educate or be educated, Hyperion returns to Greece and solitude in nature: he becomes an "Eremit" on the island of Salamis.

As a hermit, Hyperion puts the thought of rejuvenated humanity in his own time out of his mind ("ich hab ihn ausgeträumt, von Menschendingen den Traum" – p. 209), and lives for the one truth he knows – communion with the godhead of nature in which he is reunited with Diotima (p. 210).

Hermithood, in Hölderlin's *Hyperion*, is, then, the state of the prophet unheard by his people, the exponent of a nature-religion which hopes to raise mankind to a golden age of divine concord with its environment. Balked by degenerated standards with which he will not compromise, the would-be reformer seeks refuge in solitude, in consonance with the inspirational spirit of nature – there to await a rebirth, perhaps, into a humanity which may ripen in harmony with the garden producing it (p. 209) – "und ich, o Baum des Lebens, dass ich wieder grüne mit dir und deine Gipfel umatme mit all deinen knospenden Zweigen! Friedlich und innig, denn alle wuchsen wir aus dem goldnen Samenkorn herauf!"

Hyperion, as a hermit, exemplifies a certain pessimism toward society; yet, it is pessimism in a limited sense, for the firm belief in the power of nature as a religion to lift mankind to the height of its inherent potentialities is never shaken in him, only its realization is deferred to a remote future. The prophetic vision which, after repeated disappointments, looks into an unlimited vista, is positive – indeed, optimistic. Hermithood is, in *Hyperion*, characterized by underlying hope born of union with the vital elements in which the individual, the recluse, finds the spring of eternal life. The closing words of the novel: "More of this anon" ("Nächstens mehr") are to be taken in a deep and symbolic sense.

(3) In Novalis' *Heinrich von Ofterdingen*, the figure of the hermit, Friedrich von Hohenzollern, reveals the poet's peculiar gift for uniting realism with fanciful and profound symbolism; Hohenzollern embodies in his relationship to nature an uncanny perspective,

for past and future flow for him into a vast, timeless cosmos. In hermithood, he stands at the border of earthly life, where time ceases to exist, and from his vantage point he is able to evaluate the past and, to some extent, the future – he becomes a kind of genius of history.

Like Eichendorff's Don Diego and Wieland's Alfonso, Hohenzollern is an aged man with a long life rich in experience behind him. As in *Eine Meerfahrt*, the first evidence of the hermit's presence is his song, which reaches the ears of Heinrich and his party from the depth of the mountain cavern, Hohenzollern's unique hermitage. The song, itself, is an expression of the deep peace which he has found in contemplative solitude; he dwells in perfect tranquillity and consonance with nature. Divine love enriches his isolation, endowing him with a calm of spirit which is characteristic of his position on the brink between this life and the next – (p. 159) –

"Und ich steh in diesem Leben
Trunken an des Himmels Tor."

The trials and sorrows of the past (the death of his loved ones) have transfigured his earthly existence and time has ceased to have meaning for him, since he stands, as it were, between two existences – like Novalis, himself, a citizen of two worlds: still gratefully lingering in this vale, but poised for heaven – (p. 159)

"Jene lange Zahl von Tagen
Dünkt mir nur ein Augenblick;
Werd ich einst von hier getragen,
Schau ich dankbar noch zurück."

It is immediately apparent to the visitors, when they see him, that Hohenzollern is at peace with the world. Suggestive of the placid harmony in which he lives is the fact that his face is devoid of any traces of age (p. 159) – "Er sah weder alt noch jung aus." - The brightness of his glance makes it seem as though he were gazing from a mountain summit into some eternal springtime – an intimation of his capacity to perceive past and future as a cosmic whole, for he looks from this life into the next. (This characteristic has a bearing, perhaps, upon the book illustrating Heinrich's course of life and unfulfilled destiny – p. 169).

In the traditional manner, Hohenzollern is hospitable to his visitors; he is not a hermit out of misanthropy, but, rather, out of the desire to devote himself to contemplation (p. 160). For Hohenzollern (as for Alfonso and Don Diego) the life in isolation is incompatible with youth – since hermithood consists in reflection, its prerequisite is a rich fund of experience which has deepened the inner self. (The necessary tendency to strong individualism can only be developed in contact with society (p. 160). Although he had hoped to be a hermit as a young man, Hohenzollern had soon convinced himself that a youthful heart would not stand isolation.) As a young man he had felt a desire to become a hermit. This was due to the prompting of a vague but ardent enthusiasm ("heisse Schwärmerei"). He hoped and dreamed of finding full nourishment for his heart in solitude, for his inner life seemed to him an inexhaustible source. He soon realized, nevertheless, that one must bring to hermithood a wealth of experience – that a young heart cannot bear to be alone, indeed, that only through manifold experience with his kind does a man develop the independence of character, which, he implies, is requisite for hermithood (p. 160). The old miner intimates that increasing age inclines naturally toward withdrawal from society, which is generally characterized by hopefulness and a sense of common purpose, and is dedicated to activity – infancy and old age are, as a rule, shut out, since the former is a state of helplessness and the latter has seen its hope fulfilled and its purpose in life accomplished (p. 161) – "und nun nicht mehr von ihnen in den Kreis jener Gesellschaft verflochten, in sich selbst zurückkehren, und genug zu tun finden, sich auf eine höhere Gemeinschaft würdig vorzubereiten." Thus, isolation is the proper preparation for the life beyond.

Hohenzollern occupies himself by exercising in the fresh air and weaving baskets which he barters for food in nearby villages. At other times, he steeps himself in the many books which he had brought with him to the cave. Thus, he never feels discomfort or boredom in his isolation and time passes rapidly.

The gentle curiosity of the old miner – aroused probably by the rich armor (cf. *Walter*) hanging above the tombstone figures of Hohenzollern and his wife – draws out the background of the recluse who (like so many of our hermits) had been a knight. The fortunes of war had enticed the young would-be hermit into its currents, bearing him across the world to the Orient (probably in the crusades). The deaths of his children and wife had provided the immediate motivation for Hohenzollern's hermithood. Marie had died of a broken heart upon returning to Germany – and in the vicinity of the mountain cavern (p. 168). A divine illumination had come upon him and lifted the pain from his spirit, granting the peace of mind which had characterized his solitude henceforth. It is possible that the hermit feels a union with Marie and that the godly ray of light indicates that state of rapport between kindred souls in the heart of nature (cf. Hiebel, *Novalis*, p. 280).

The epitaph on the side of the tomb reads (p. 161) – "Friedrich und Marie von Hohenzollern kehrten auf dieser Stelle in ihr Vaterland zurück." The word, "Vaterland" refers, without doubt, not only to the scene of Marie's (and Hohenzollern's eventual) death, but to the cavern, itself, and its symbolic properties. In the remote depth of the mountain, as it is, the cavern suggests the innermost heart of nature, where time almost does not exist for the hermit; here, past and future, earthly life and that of the spirit, blend into one another and are inseparable. In intimacy with the core of nature, then, Hohenzollern is master of an unusual perspective; he becomes the exponent of the apotheosis of history – a poetic history which presents the past in the light of the future. Heinrich's encounter with the hermit occurs in the architectural center (fifth chapter of nine) of the first part of the novel. As a ripening poet, he experiences and absorbs into himself all that he witnesses. Hohenzollern, consequently, performs what we have called an "educational" function. He imparts an interpretation of history, which is based upon the timeless, unified perspective, to which we previously referred, and which is his special property as a hermit, as we have seen (p. 162) – "Der eigentliche Sinn für die Geschichten der Menschen entwickelt sich erst spät, und mehr unter den stillen Einflüssen der Erinnerung, als unter den gewaltsameren Eindrücken der Gegenwart. Die nächsten Ereignisse scheinen nur locker verknüpft, aber sie sympathisieren desto wunderbarer mit entfernteren; nur dann, wenn man imstande ist, eine lange Reihe zu übersehn und weder alles buchstäblich zu nehmen, noch auch mit mutwilligen Träumen die eigentliche Ordnung zu verwirren, bemerkt man die geheime Verkettung des Ehemaligen und Künftigen, und lernt die Geschichte aus Hoffnung und Erinnerung zusammensetzen." The hermit's exposition, here, is based upon his wide experience prior to isolation; he analyzes the development and character of the perspective (as we have already seen) which distinguishes his state in hermithood – in addition (and primarily, of course) it is his conception of history. What he had maintained concerning hermithood, Hohenzollern, naturally, applies to the historical concept – that is – it should be written, not by the young but by old reverent folk, who have no further history of their own left to live and who await only their transplantation to the heavenly garden (p. 162). The technique of unrolling facts is not the goal, but, rather, the poetic revelation of truth (p. 164) – "Es ist mehr Wahrheit in ihren (the poets') Märchen, als in gelehrten Chroniken."

The hermit had learned his interpretation of history, had acquired his marvelous perspective, from communion with nature in the cavern abode (p. 165) – "Seitdem ich in dieser Höhle wohne, –, habe ich mehr über die alte Zeit nachdenken gelernt. – Wenn ich mir die wilde Zeit denke, wo diese fremdartigen, ungeheuren Tiere in dichten Scharen sich in diese Höhlen hereindrängten, von Furcht und Angst vielleicht getrieben, und hier ihren Tod fanden; wenn ich dann wieder bis zu den Zeiten hinaufsteige, wo diese Höhlen zusammenwuchsen und ungeheure Fluten das Land bedeckten: so komme ich mir selbst wie ein Traum der Zukunft, wie ein Kind des ewigen Friedens vor."

As an example (although not designated as such) of the ideal history, the strange book which seems to portray his life and experiences, past and future, falls into the hands of the fascinated Heinrich (p. 169): it represents the course of his life and all those persons with whom he had come into contact, together with others as yet unknown to him – Mathilde and Klingsohr. The unfamiliar scenes are quite obviously the experiences of the future and the missing conclusion points toward the after-life.

The past of Novalis' hermit, Hohenzollern, is transformed in his relationship to nature and blended with the future; in isolation, the last stage of life, he becomes a citizen of two worlds gifted with a strange perspective – past, present, and future are, in his eyes, one eternity. As its prophet, he is the spirit of poetic history.

(4) The hermit in Schiller's *Die Braut von Messina* is endowed by nature (and God) with mystic power to recognize the changing direction of fate; like Hohenzollern, he, too, has insight into future events by virtue of his age (1. 2099) and his communion with nature. He had his hermitage on the lofty crags of Mt. Etna; known as "der Greis des Berges" he has been there since time immemorial.

Great importance is attributed here, also, to the location of the hermit's abode. Since he exists aloof from ordinary folk on the rocky heights near to heaven, he is considered to be in intimate contact with the divine forces governing the destinies of men. As a holy man whose senses have been purified by the rarer breezes, he possesses the character of a seer. Because of the perspective from his remote dwelling, his insight into life is deeper than that of others –

(1. 2103-2105)   "Und von dem Berg der aufgewälzten Jahre
                    Hinabsieht in das aufgelöste Spiel
                    Des unverständlich krummgewundnen Lebens."

The solitary holy man possesses knowledge of the fate which hangs over the house of Messina and which is embodied in Isabella's daughter, Beatrice. At Isabella's behest, he had frequently used his extraordinary power to avert evil destiny by prayer.

Isabella had sent a messenger to the hermit to discover the whereabouts of her daughter who had disappeared from the cloister. The recluse sends back word that she has been found by Don Manuel. When he receives the candle, presented by Isabella as a token of gratitude, instead of lighting it in honor of his saint, the frenzied hermit sets fire to his hut, and disappears, crying portentously three times, "Wehe!"

To be sure, the audience, or reader, knows, prior to this scene, that Manuel has been killed by his brother and that his corpse will subsequently be brought into the palace. The behavior of the hermit represents horror, for he foresees the terrible fulfillment of the curse in the discovery of Beatrice. The function of the report concerning him is certainly to add a degree of suspense and to emphasize the fate which is about to fall upon the noble house.

The conception of the hermit praying to avert a curse and of his violent reaction of horror to its imminence, as revealed in the destruction of his hermitage, would suggest, perhaps, a strong pagan, or Asiatic, coloring (which is, on the other hand, not incompatible to the mixture of pagan and Christian elements throughout the tragedy – expecially the interpretation of fate).

The salient characteristic, however, is the interpretation of the hermit as possessing unusual, supernatural insight into life and into its subjection to the powers of fate – all of which he derives from the perspective inherent in his vantage point on the remote mountain peak where the air breathed by ordinary men is thinned to the ether of the suprarational realm.

(5) The figure of the hermit, Paul, in Uhland's dramatic fragment, *König Eginhard*, also known as *Schildeis* contributes little of additional interest to our consideration of the relationship of the recluse to nature, but the poet's charming treatment of him merits a brief discussion here. The most important aspect is the fact that the hermit, for Uhland, represents the strong romantic attachment to the forest – a love which becomes a salient characteristic not only of German Romanticism, but of German literature henceforth. Paul is conceived as a semi-comic character (cf. also Düntzer, *Uhlands Dramen und Dramenentwürfe*, p. 80-81 –), whose sermons on human life and nature have a tedious effect on the old knight, Dietwald, but whose discourses on the forest are to be taken in all earnest. The material of the fragment is drawn from a folk tale, included by the Grimm brothers in their *Deutsche Sagen* (p. 204, footnote) and the figure of the hermit is taken over by Uhland from the traditional legend (cf. also Düntzer – p. 39).

Eginhard has fled with his abducted bride, Adelheit, Emperor Otto's daughter, and seeks refuge in the ancient castle, Schildeis, hidden deep in the recesses of the Bohemian Forest – it had been the hunting castle of Eginhard's father many years earlier. In the forest near the castle, Eginhard and Adelheit, accompanied by Dietwald, meet the hermit, who guides them to their destination, inhabited only by the venerable "Burgvogt," Eckart (also from the tale). The latter has literally lost track of time, and takes the young Eginhard for his long deceased father.

Only the hermit is intimately acquainted with the timelessness of the retreat. Here, surrounded by forest and cliff, he feels no hint of passing time and life in the world outside goes on without intruding upon his "Waldeinsamkeit."

Loneliness and intimacy with the environment make the hermit sensitive to the spirit life which frequents the castle. There at midnight, the ghosts of its former lords wander through the halls –

(p. 206) "Sie kehren gerne zu dem Haus zurück,
Wo alles noch ist wie zu ihrer Zeit."

The recluse explains that the changeless atmosphere of Schildeis and of the thick forest about it have made his only human contact, the old Eckart, forget his age completely. In Uhland's fragment as in Novalis' *Heinrich von Ofterdingen*, the hermit is characterized by the sense of timelessness. Uhland's hermit finds this quality specifically in the "Wald" typical, as we have seen, for the German "Einsiedel" and here, especially, for Swabian Romanticism. The forest becomes for Paul a symbol of this timelessness –

(p. 207) "Den Wechsel selbst der Jahreszeiten lässt
Der Tannenwälder ewig Dunkelgrün,
Der Felsen ewig frühlingslose Öde
In unsrer Wildnis weniger bemerken."

Isolation from the world makes the recluse talkative and the arrival of Eginhard and his party inspire the hermit to a sermon on life which reveals the specific source of comfort for him in the forest of Schildeis. The seasonal cycles in nature ordinarily become a taunt for man whose life is a brief blossoming followed by prolonged withering. The youth is saddened by the bareness of autumn which foreshadows the coming of old age, while spring occasions pain for those (like Paul) bowed with years –

(p. 207) "Da will des Greises Wange neu sich röten,
Sich zu verjüngen meint das matte Herz.
Ach, kurze Täuschung nur!"

Thus, human life is interpreted by the hermit in terms of nature – in the comparison, however, man must be saddened by the long and single direction of his cycle. Therefore, the hermit finds consolation in the timeless forest of his solitude –

(p. 207) "Drum lob' ich diese wechsellose Gegend,
Wo nichts im Herzen weckt der Sehnsucht Qual."

Here, where it has been untouched by time and where man no longer sets his foot, the forest represents earth in the early stages of creation. The elements seem as yet unseparated. Since no light falls through upon the chaos of cliffs and ravines, even the plants are lacking. Dark waters rush beneath the rocks and clouds lie in the gorges – the forest is the symbol of all natural forces combined – the portrait of life fresh from the hand of the creator. In this atmosphere and in the isolation of hermithood, the solitary often feels a primeval, divine strength surge through him and he calls through the vast silence "Es werde!" – the timelessness of the forest and its revelation of pristine forces in the creation let the hermit experience the power of the Godhead in contrast with the impotent voice of man.

The poet smiles, to be sure, at the grandiosity of his hermit's inspiration – at his glowing eye and fluttering locks. The humour, nevertheless, which is implied, particularly in the closing lines of Paul's "Schöpfungserlebnis" (p. 208) is sympathetic.

The forest represents, ultimately, for the hermit (and Romanticism) nature, undisturbed by man, removed from time (as does Don Diego's island in *Meerfahrt*) –

(p. 208)   "Die weiten, stillen Wälder, wo der Mensch,
Des Schöpfers letztes Werk, noch fehlt,
Und dort noch in der Ferne das Gebirg,
Das liegt nun vollends ausser aller Zeit."

Hermithood embodies, here, love for the forest as a symbol, too, of the timeless essence of the "Heimat;" although this connotation is nowhere specifically suggested in the lines, an unmistakable feeling of it surges beneath the surface of much of the verse given to the recluse.

(6) The designation of the hermit as "Waldvater" in Kerner's "Märchendichtung," *Die Heimatlosen* indicates two important features of the figure. For Kerner, "Wald" is nature, a living, universal spirit, while "Vater" suggests the supremacy of this spirit and the intimate relationship of it to all beings; the "Waldvater," then, is the fatherly spirit governing and pervading all life – the figure of the hermit is identified (more conclusively than in Bürger's *Der wilde Jäger*) with nature, itself. Another tenet inherent in the tale is of the utmost significance – one upon which the interpretation of the hermit figure (or of the tale) must be based. The concept of "Todessehnsucht" is a longing for reunion with the spirit of nature – for reunification with nature, itself. For Kerner, this longing or drive, is natural and inherent in all beings.

After having first read the tale, Uhland wrote to his friend (*Justinus Kerners Briefwechsel mit seinen Freunden*, Bd. 1, p. 338-339) – asking the question, "Sind es nur solche bewusstlose Prophezeiungen, krankhafte Ahnungen, zwecklose Zerrüttungen, was man im innigeren Umgang mit der Natur gewinnt – ?" In his answer (cf. previous reference, p. 340-343), Kerner explained his conception of

"Todessehnsucht" or reunification with nature; his explanation, of course, derives from his experience as a physician – this biographical fact had much stronger influences upon Kerner's poetic world than is generally conceded or recognized. Death is the most intimate union with the spirit of nature and every type of sickness is a striving toward this union – organic decay in any part of the body, even the sensitivity of scars to atmospheric changes are circumstances which bring the individual into more intimate contact with the nature spirit. The completely healthy body acts as a bulwark against such reunification. Dispositions which reveal an unusual inclination toward intimacy with the secrets of nature (and Kerner compares Novalis with Serpentin) are destined for early union to it.

We have referred very briefly, in connection with the hermit of *Oberon*, to the symbolism of the sea as a representation of eternity. This idea is implicit in Kerner's tale; at the conclusion of Sililie's "Märchen" which introduces the story and to which Serpentin listens in a dream-like state (much as Ofterdingen's dream of the blue flower introduces Novalis' novel), Goldener, after long wandering, is crowned by fisher-folk, and gazes from a ship decked with flowers toward the sun sinking into the sea (p. 281) and Serpentin, himself, falls asleep dreaming of the burning sun upon the waves (the tale was originally entitled "Die Wanderer zum Morgenrot").

We learn from the Count (p. 302) of "Waldvaters" history; he had been born on the barren, rocky island, Helgoland, and spent his youth in play by the ocean which surrounded his home. Later he became a seaman. Having returned from a long voyage, he had discovered (as did Joseph in *Godwi*) that his wife, convinced of his death at sea had remarried. The shock apparently led to his hermithood. The curious nature of the life and background of "Waldvater" is almost lost in legend and the strange saga-like atmosphere surrounding his life lends him an air of mystery in keeping with his symbolic value. Of his past otherwise, nothing is known but that he had retreated to hermithood in a remote mountain forest – the same forest, of course, to which his great-great-grandchildren, Serpentin and Sililie, had been brought with their older brother, Luchs (p. 286).

The description of the hermit's appearance (p. 283) is designed to suggest his personification of the spirit of the wild forest surrounding his cabin. The hair of head and chin is like moss. Bent and twisted, and having skin which is leathern and wrinkled, he has the aspect of one of the ancient roots which supply part of his diet. He is "uralt," and has inhabited the cabin as long as can be remembered. The fact that the strange master of nature-cures, Lambert, dwells in the same cabin is an intimation of the source of the latter's capacities and an additional hint as to the identification of "Waldvater." We have mentioned the eternal significance of the sea; the turtle which "Waldvater" carries in his gnarled fingers is further evidence of his timeless source – the aged turtle is the same as that which appears in the portraits in the Count's castle (p. 296-297) of "Waldvater" as a child and as a seaman.

The hermit's death and burial convey actually, not his reunification to nature, but, rather, his utter identification with it. He is buried in a stalactite cavern by Lambert, Sililie, and the mountain folk, to whom he had been known as "Waldvater, Geist dieser alten Wälder" – henceforth he will be "Geist der Wasser, Metalle und Gesteine dieser Gebirge" (p. 300). The properties of the waters which drip from the cave walls preserve his body (cf. also Hoffmann's *Bergwerke zu Falun*, where the hero also had been a seaman, and Eichendorff's *Eine Meerfahrt*: in both, the removal from time is a strong theme as here, and in Uhland's Paul). In death, his hands have the texture of the turtle's shell (which split at the moment of the old man's decease), his neck is like the bark of an ancient tree overgrown with moss, and the crystal-bright eyes have opened like dew-pearls on a water-lily. The entire ceremony of burial is a strange, beautiful rite of nature and the song of the maidens, which accompanies his interment in the cavern, celebrates his eternal preservation (p. 301) –

> "Erglüh mit dem Kristall der Kluft,
> Du Aug' mit hellem Schein,
> Einst finde man in Felsen dich
> Als reichen Edelstein."

The relationship of "Waldvater" to Sililie, Serpentin, and Luchs, his great-great-grandchildren, lends to the tale a kind of allegorical quality – nature and its children constitute one large family. The circumstances of the actual family history (p. 301-304), which separated the hermit, originally, from his wife, and the subsequent shipwreck of the parents of Serpentin, Sililie and Luchs, give the tale its title, "Die Heimatlosen" (the theme of which is expressed in Luchs' "Die Strassen, die ich gehe"). All three offspring long inwardly for the "Heimat," which is the eternal spirit of nature. Serpentin is tempted by the visions of light inspired through Sililie's "Märchen" (p. 281), a preview of his own course of life, to leave the dark forests in search of the "Morgenrot." Sililie, of course, does not wander forth; as a female, she exists in more intimate communion with nature than do her brothers ("und eilt auch bälder als der Mann den gänzlichen Verein mit der Natur, dem Tode, zu" – *Briefwechsel*, Bd. 1, p. 341). Her suprarational understanding of the sensitive child (p. 286-287) which exhibits such closeness to nature and is, therefore, soon united to it, reveals the feminine receptivity to the secrets of the pervading spirit – Sililie's nearness to the spirit of nature is most strongly suggested by her care for "Waldvater," shortly before his "death," as well as by his pleasurable reaction to her (p. 295). Luchs (Kerner's version of Goethe's "Harfner") is obsessed by the same urge to wander in search of eternal dawn as is his brother, Serpentin.

Serpentin and Sililie succumb to their inner longing immediately after the burial of "Waldvater." In her dying hour, Sililie, like Serpentin, envisions eternal light, while Luchs, of more vigorous constitution than his sensitive brother and sister, is doomed to endless wandering in search of his "Heimat" – he is seized by the urge to set out again (p. 307) at the time of Serpentin's final sickness. From the distance, the tones of his harp and song enter Serpentin's chamber, while a magnificent sunrise fires the sky –

(p. 307) "Doch fern Gebirge ragen,
Die meine Heimat tragen,
Ein ewig Morgenrot."

Kerner's hermit, therefore, is a "Sagengestalt", more properly a symbol or personification of the nature-spirit, rather than a person. The poet uses his hermit, who draws his progeny after him to eternal life, as an exponent of "Todessehnsucht" and reunification with nature – the "Waldvater" is nature, taking unto himself its family.

(7) Goethe also puts the hermit figure to symbolic use in the final scene of *Faust* – to a use quite different, however, from Kerner's. It is of importance to note that Goethe uses, specifically, four anchorites – not ordinary hermits. We recall (cf. also definitions in the Introduction) that the anchorite, unlike the hermit, takes a vow of utter seclusion, and is committed to the most severe isolation for the remainder of his life. The ties with earthly life are severed forever; there is no turning back and only his body still binds him to this world, for his entire soul is directed toward the next.

The portion of the final scene containing the "heilige Anachoreten" (1. 11844-12103) acts, in a sense, as a sort of prelude to the arrival of Faust's soul into the sphere of eternal love. The anchorites represent stages of spiritualization in nature ("Naturvergeistigung"), which free the soul of its transitory physical properties that it may enter into the pure sphere of love emanating from the presence of the "Mater gloriosa," "das Ewig-Weibliche."

The site of the anchorites' hermitages is probably modeled after Montserat (north of Barcelona) in Spain ("mons serratus" or jagged mountain) which contained a monastery and countless anchorite cells; it was the goal of over 6,000 pilgrims a year, and was sacred to the Virgin. It is also possible that Goethe was partly inspired by descriptions of a Pisan Fresco (df. *Sämtliche Werke*, Bd. 14, p. 401

and Schröer, *Goethes Faust II*, p. 381), which portrays the lions (1. 11850) –

        "Löwen, sie schleichen stumm –
        Freundlich um uns herum –."

The quiet, friendly beasts, transformed by the sacred nature of the hermitage, (as also in Dürer's St. Jerome engraving) are traditional symbols of the pervading power of love.

(1. 11852)   "Ehren geweihten Ort,
                   Heiligen Liebeshort."

The anchorites are situated in cells at varying levels, according to the stages of "Vergeistigung", in the rocky cliff which rises out of the plain. Of the four anchorites, the Pater ecstaticus is not stationary; he represents the most transitional state of spiritualization through his continuous hovering up and down past the cells of the other three. In him, the poet reveals the emotion and inner working of the power of love in nature, which dissipates the last elements of the physical, leaving the essence of love, itself, the soul –

(1. 11862-11865) "Dass ja das Nichtige
                    Alles verflüchtige,
                    Glänze der Dauerstern,
                    Ewiger Liebe Kern."

As his designation implies, the Pater ecstaticus embodies in the intensity of the verses allotted to him the extreme ecstasy of "Vergeistigung" (ecstasy – in mystical language, a psychological state in which intense mental absorption in divine things is accompanied by loss of sense perception and voluntary control – to put out of place, from Greek *existanai*): the fact, too, that he is in motion indicates his complete spirituality – he is all emotion; his stage will be reached by each of his brothers.

   The second anchorite, Pater profundus, is closest to the substantial elements of nature. He is aware of the rushing streams plunging eventually into larger rivers and the mighty energy which projects tree trunks into the air – all these possess a driving strength generated by love, the motivating force of nature, which is evident in all elements –

(1. 11873)   "So ist es die allmächtige Liebe
                 Die alles bildet, alles hegt."

The roaring waters from the mountain irrigate the fields and the lightning flames purify the air –

(1. 11882)   "Sind Liebesboten, sie verkünden,
                 Was ewig schaffend uns umwallt."

This anchorite wishes to derive inspiration from the loving force which permeates nature as he feels it – the source of spiritualization is, for him, in the substances of earth –

(1. 11884) "Mein Innres mög' es auch entzünden,
Wo sich der Geist, verworren, kalt,
Verquält in stumpfer Sinne Schranken,
Scharfangeschlossnem Kettenschmerz."

Pater seraphicus, as opposed to the Pater profundus, is in a higher cell as befits his state; he is almost free of the physical. In him, spirituality is in ascendancy over matter and, consequently, he is receptive to the spirit world. The fine nuance of transition from physical to spiritual is disclosed in the anchorite's perception of the souls of midnight children – those children born at the spirit hour are, according to tradition, fated for untimely death. As a tiny morning cloud hovers over the pines and floats closer, the anchorite is aware of the children-spirits, who, because of early death, have not known nature in earthly life. They pass into the eyes of the Pater, and, through him, perceive the wonders of earth.[1] The Pater seraphicus releases them, and, in turn, is able to follow their flight into the realms of pure spirit – this instance, too, reveals the infinite power of love, for it is through this universal-natural emotion that the anchorite has contact with the spiritual –

(1. 11902) "Dass ein Liebender zugegen,
Fühlt ihr wohl, so naht euch nur!"

The Doctor Marianus, who is in the loftiest cell, enjoys the ultimate state of spiritualization which is possible in this life; therefore, it is given to him to perceive the presence of the Mater gloriosa, "das Ewig-Weibliche." He is able to witness the forgiveness of the four women sinners, Maria Magdalena, the Samaritan woman, Maria of Egypt, and Gretchen; all four had committed sins of the flesh, of nature, and all four obtain mercy. Doctor Marianus, of course, comprehends the ascension of Faust's soul through Gretchen's love and intercession for grace. Therefore, to Doctor Marianus are given the final verses, prior to those of the mystic choir which sums up the theme of the scene and of the poem. As an anchorite in the final stage of spiritualization, he testifies for mankind to the miracle of redemption through love –

(1. 12096) "Blicket auf zum Retterblick,
Alle reuig Zarten
Euch zu seligem Geschick
Dankend umzuarten."

[1] The almost certain source for this entire conception of the "midnight children" is to be found in Klopstock's *Messias*, I, 1. 652 ff.

In the figures of his anchorites, Goethe portrays compositely hermithood as the border existence between the earthly and spiritual worlds; in each of his individual figures, as we have seen, he graduates the extent of spiritualization, making his last anchorite witness to the supreme mystery of redemption through love – the eternal power which pervades all of nature. Although these anchorites are occupied with religious rites (unlike the others of this chapter), religion and love are bound to the conception of nature.[1]

(8) Don Diego, the hermit of Eichendorff's *Eine Meerfahrt* combines orthodox religion with harmony in nature; as a hermit, he embodies heroic qualities. His natural piety saves him from temptation of the flesh and his hermithood represents a triumph over life –, the termination of a stormy career in placid concord with nature and God. Diego conforms to the tradition of knightly, adventurous "Einsiedler" – as do Trevrizent, Hohenzollern, and, particularly, Alfonso in *Oberon*, who is also Spanish, and finds peace on a remote and rocky island.

Although his hermithood is partially the result of victory through divine aid over dangerous passion, we may consider it, in a sense, his natural goal in life. As he tells Antonio, Alvarez, and Alma of the outset of his portentous voyage, he describes his dream-empire (p. 347) – "Ich war damals noch jung, vor meiner Seele dämmerte bei Tag und Nacht ein wunderbares Reich mit blühenden Inseln und goldenen Türmen aus den Fluten herauf –." In response to his ill-fated Lieutenant's belief that it is foolhardy to seek Eldorado in the world, since it lies upon the seas of eternity, Diego insists that he must try, or else resign himself to never finding it (p. 348). The implications are clear – only he has the right to dwell in an ideal realm, who has the strength of will to conquer it for himself, to earn it by service and trimph over the trials of life (as Diego tells Antonio, too, before parting from him.) To be sure there is also some truth in Lieutenant Alonzo's contention that it lies in eternity, for Diego's Eldorado turns out to be an empire rich in the eternal peace of God and nature.

To earn his right to the island hermitage of tranquillity and concord, Diego must first trimph over the dangers and temptations of its evil and pagan counterpart, the island of the passionate (Penthesilea-type) warrior queen (cf. also Ulmer, *Eichendorff's Eine Meerfahrt*, p. 151). It is, however, Diego's piety which (together with the miracle of his escape from the flaming ship) helps him survive the evils of the queen and her exotic, savage island kingdom. On the dawn of the day on which Diego and his party land, the island seems

---

[1] To be sure, these stages of spiritualization through nature represented in the anchorites imply the final attenuation of Faust, himself.

to be bathed in the morning light of the Lord's angel, who stands with flaming sword on the mountain peak driving the original sinners from paradise (p. 348-349). The picture which enters Diego's mind suggests to the reader the atmosphere of the tempting, sinister beauty of the island and its queen and, at the same time, the hand of divine providence which is to shield the adventurous young man. Although in eventual close contact he is fascinated by the savage queen's beauty – "nun fesselte mich ihre Schönheit, und ganz verwirrt und geblendet drückte ich flüchtig ihre Hand" (p. 354) – he never succumbs to her wild charm as does his Lieutenant Alonzo. The latter becomes her slave completely, deserting his company and ending in madness – keeping watch by the preserved body of his witch-goddess (cf. Kerner – theme of preservation) until his death at the hands of Antonio and his party (p. 330). When Diego swears, however, to convert the queen and rule the island in God's name or never to return to Europe, he falls into the deepest temptation, for he is, in truth, dangerously near to becoming the victim of his passion (p. 356) – "Ich Tor, ich bildete mir ein, den Himmel zu erobern, und meinte doch nur das schöne Weib!" Yet, through divine intervention, he survives the exploding ship's magazine, (which destroys the source of temptation) and the ordeal adrift on the waves; he is washed ashore on the true island paradise – where he hangs his sword on a tree (Antonio sees it overgrown symbolically with blossoms) and becomes a hermit, devoted entirely to God, his benefactor, and the peace of His nature.

As a hermit, Diego has come through the trials of violent adventure and temptation; with the death of the island queen and his own providential escape from death, he assumes in hermithood a greatness of proportion commensurate with the fullness of the life behind him and with the eternal concord which characterizes his saintly solitude. Near his hermitage, Diego has cultivated a garden above which, on the mountainside, there stands a cross. The garden is symbolic of the hermit's accord with God and nature – an expression of his devotion and piety (cf. also Ulmer, *Eichendorff's Eine Meerfahrt* – p. 150).

The heroic aspect of the hermit, derived from his trimph over life and temptation and from his background of enterprise and adventure, is frequently accentuated by the poet. On the evening following the landing on Diego's island, a soldier reports to Antonio and Alvarez his having seen the gigantic figure of a saint standing on a peak (p. 340) – "Die ersten Abendsterne am Firmament hatten das Haupt des Bildes wie ein Heiligenschein umgeben –." The figure is, of course, immediately identified as the gardener whom they had previously assumed to be "der liebe Gott selber" – (p. 339). When Diego appears, he creates again the same awe-inspiring impression

(p. 342) – "ein schöner, riesenhafter Greis mit langem, weissem Bart, in rauhem Fell gekleidet, eine brennende Fackel in der Hand–." (costume here and the motif of footprints seen earlier are reminiscent of Robinson Crusoe). The song which heralds his appearance (like that of Hohenzollern) sums up his transcendence over past life; the years, which have floated by like clouds, have left him in peaceful solitude (p. 341) –

> "Die Jahre wie die Wolken gehn
> Und lassen mich hier einsam stehn,
> Die Welt hat mich vergessen,
> Da tratst du wunderbar zu mir,
> Wenn ich bei Waldesrauschen hier
> In stiller Nacht [1] gesessen."

It is interesting that Don Diego's song is a variation of Grimmelshausen's hermit in Simplicissimus (Book I, Chap. 7), beginning "Komm, Trost der Nacht, o Nachtigal!" Both hermits are heard singing the songs which characterize their states of existence before they are seen. Grimmelshausen's hermit expresses a typically strong "jenseitig" urge; his nightingale praises God in heaven. For Don Diego, on the other hand, the longing for eternity is imbued, typically, with "Naturfrömmigkeit" and his spiritual longing finds intimacy and union with the nature spirit personified as Night. The two poems form an interesting contrast between one of our earliest hermit figures (Baroque) and our final one, Eichendorff's Don Diego – who, in spite of affinities with his predecessor, is most typically romantic.

Although it is literally not true that the world had forgotten him (he lives in song and Antonio has come to seek information about him), the tone of the verses conveys the peace which is his in solitude, when the presence of God comes to him through the night-rustling of the trees.

The sense of loftiness, which we have already noticed in the appearance of the hermit on the ridge and silhouetted on the mountain peak, implies not only his superior position over the life of action brought to a tranquil close, but also (as in the instance of the cross above the garden) his nearness to God and the next life. This aspect is apparent also at close range. When Antonio falls upon his knees before Diego at the conclusion of the story which identifies him as the young man's uncle, the venerable hermit's long white beard envelops him "wie Höhenrauch" (p. 363).

---

[1] Most published versions of the poem have this line as "Gedankenvoll gesessen" – a version which seems more logical, since the verses are addressed to Night (cf. Walter Silz, *German Romantic Lyrics*, p. 63 – Harvard University Press, 1934).

Diego gives his blessing to Alma as well as to Antonio, for, in her, he recognizes the virtuous, loving counterpart of her aunt, the island queen – what had not been granted to him, will be fulfilled for Antonio. The advice given to Antonio before his departure for Spain sums up Diego's philosophy of life and hermithood. As in *Heinrich von Ofterdingen* and *Oberon*, the hermit's existence is not for the young; the duty of youth consists in winning spurs in the battle of life. Only by successful struggle can the individual hope to attain the rock of spiritual tranquility, on which the storms of life are shattered (p. 366) – "Mein Leben ist wie ein Gewitter schön und schrecklich vorübergezogen, und die Blitze spielen nur noch fern am Horizont wie in eine andere Welt hinüber."

Hermithood represents, then, for Eichendorff, the refuge in God and nature of the active, adventurous man who has successfully withstood the storms and temptations of life; from his remote vantage point, he (like Wieland's Alfonso and Novalis' Hohenzollern) gains a profound perspective through which (as Diego does in his narrative) he may evaluate his experience in the light of the next world. For the hermit, earthly life has passed like a storm, leaving only distant lightning flashes on the horizon of eternity. Hermithood, to Eichendorff's religious mind, appears as a twilight zone of spiritual preparation interposed between the setting of the "diesseitige Welt" and the dawn of an unending "Jenseits."

Eichendorff's positive and profound portrayal of the hermit concludes our discussion of the recluse in his relationship to nature.

In the initial portions of our study, the hermit retreated from society for a great variety of reasons – most of them constituted revolt against an accepted set of standards of living. In our second chapter, specifically, the majority of works belonged to "Sturm und Drang," a movement embodying and glorifying the revolt of the individualist. The third chapter treated of purely subjective problems; predominant among these was the tragic love experience, which required in hermithood adjustment to a new reality – isolation was the medium in which the recluse sought peace of mind by recreating from within himself such a new reality. Biographically speaking, our concluding chapter portrays the hermit's relationship to that reality found in isolation, the world of nature; it is not surprising, therefore, that the works involved represented Romanticism, where nature is the very medium of spiritualization.

As we have seen, through nature the hermit becomes aware of his eternal, universal destiny. In nature, he finds the revelation of a kindred spirit to which he is reunited and in the cycles of which he recognizes a principle of immortality – here is his most characteristically individual role, for hermithood is extreme individualism and the hermit embodies man, who is never in his life so alone as upon the threshold of eternity.

No figure or type, recurrently appearing in German literature, reveals to such a degree the inwardness, the inner experiencing of the most basic problems in human existence. The hermit stands on an invisible frontier between everyday strife and the absolute, and views life from a vantage point which places all relationships in a universally valid perspective.

The selection of the period from Lessing to Eichendorff was not arbitrary, for during the movements of Enlightenment, Storm and Stress, Classicism, and Romanticism, which partly coincide with, and overlap one another, the hermit figure appears in a particularly rich variety of interpretations and works.

Yet, he does not become extinct as the nineteenth century progresses, but continues to turn up with not-so-surprising regularity. Without attempting to be comprehensive, we suggest a few typical examples.

In Stifter's *Der Hochwald*, Gregor, the venerable "Jäger," dwelling in the isolation of dense forest, embodies the spirit of timeless nature in much the same manner as Kerner's "Waldvater." Scheffel's *Ekkehard* withdraws to icy Alpine peaks to find inspiration and a source of vital strength. The principal figure in Storm's *Bulemanns Haus* is an unorthodox hermit-miser who shuts himself off from the world out of misanthropy; he is done to death by his two supernatural cats. Nietzsche's Zarathrustra is (like Hyperion) an uncompromising idealist aspiring to raise up and rejuvenate mankind.

In literature of the twentieth century, Gerhart Hauptmann's pseudo-hermit in *Der Ketzer von Soana* forms his own religion in a pagan world of creative nature, while Rembrandt in Erwin Guido Kolbenheyer's *Amor Dei*, withdraws into a mysterious darkness like that of his own later paintings – embodying a relationship between isolation and art (remotely reminiscent of that in Brentano's *Godwi*). Orla, in Wiechert's *Das einfache Leben*, retires from despair over the chaos in life to an island in East Prussia, where, occupying himself with manual labor, he ponders the nature of God. The hermithood of Josephus Famulus in Hesse's *Das Glasperlenspiel* represents withdrawal based on general disgust for life which is the evidence of slackening faith.

It is not surprising that several lyric poets of the present century have seen fit to adopt the hermit-pose. Stefan George's *Der Einsiedel* is a traditional medieval hermit, who (like Eichendorff's Don Diego or Wolfram's Trevrizent) watches a young man (here, his son) depart to struggle with life. Rudolf Alexander Schröder poses as a hermit in the final poem of his cycle, *Die Ballade vom Wanders-*

mann. Having rid himself of all ties to wordly life, he contemplates eternity from the vantage point of a windswept ridge.

It is fitting that we close our study with brief mention of Georg Trakl's poem, *An die Verstummten*. The poet enumerates with prophetic vision the vices and materialism which have plagued our era, and made a chaos of human life. For him, above all, the cycles of nature persuade of order and immortality, albeit he is most sensitive to its decadent aspect. He concludes with the lines –

"Aber stille blutet in dunkler Höhle stummere Menschheit,
Fügt aus harten Metallen das erlösende Haupt."

Thus, here too, at the outset of our century, the hermit becomes (like Hölderlin's Hyperion) the apotheosis of the isolated individual, suffering out of love for humanity under standards of life with which he will not compromise – yet embodying undying hope for redemption in the future.

CHRONOLOGICAL TABLE OF WORKS
IN ALL PARTS OF THIS STUDY

(Roman numerals following titles indicate the Chapter of
the study in which a work appears.)

1749 – Lessing – Der Eremit II
1773 – Goethe – Satyros II
1775 – Goethe – Erwin und Elmire (cf. 1787) III
       Lenz – Die Kleinen II
1776 – Klinger – Die Zwillinge III
       Klinger – Sturm und Drang II
       Lenz – Der Waldbruder III
1778 – Bürger – Der wilde Jäger II
1779 – Lessing – Nathan der Weise II
1780 – Wieland – Oberon IV
1787 – Goethe – Erwin und Elmire (second version) III
1791 – Klinger – Fausts Leben (etc) III
1799 – Wackenroder – Ein wunderbares Märchen von einem nackten Heiligen III
       Hölderlin – Hyperion IV
1800 – Brentano – Godwi III
1801 – Novalis – Heinrich von Ofterdingen IV
1803 – Schiller – Die Braut von Messina IV
1809 – Uhland – König Eginhard (Schildeis) IV
1811 – Kerner – Die Heimatlosen IV
1813 – Chamisso – Peter Schlemihl II
1817 – Hoffmann – Serapion III
1818 – Droste-Hülshoff – Walter III
1832 – Goethe – Faust IV
       Lenau – Die Marionetten IV
1835 – Eichendorff – Eine Meerfahrt IV

BIBLIOGRAPHY

I - *Texts*

BRENTANO, CLEMENS - *Godwi* - herausgegeben und eingeleitet von Anselm Ruest - Berlin, n.d.

BÜRGER, GOTTFRIED AUGUST - *Gedichte* - herausgegeben von August Sauer (Deutsche National-Literatur, Bd. 78) Berlin und Stuttgart, n.d.

CHAMISSO, ADELBERT VON - *Werke*, 2 Bde. herausgegeben von Hermann Tardel - Bibliographisches Institut, Leipzig und Wien, n.d.
Werke - herausgegeben von Oskar Walzel (Deutsche National-Literatur, Bd. 148) Stuttgart, n.d.

DROSTE-HÜLSHOFF, Annette von - *Sämtliche Werke*, 4 Bde. In Verbindung mit Bertha Badt herausgegeben von Karl Schulte-Kemminghausen - Georg Müller, München, 1930.

EICHENDORFF, JOSEPH, FREIHERR VON - *Gedichte, Erzählungen, Biographisches* - ausgewählt und eingeleitet von Max Wehrli - Atlantis, Zürich, 1945.

ESCHENBACH, WOLFRAM VON - *Parzival und Titurel*, 3 Bde. - herausgegeben von Karl Bartsch (Deutsche Classiker des Mittelalters, Bde. IX, X, XI) Brockhaus, Leipzig, 1875.

GOETHE, JOHANN WOLFGANG VON - *Sämtliche Werke*, Jubiläums - Ausgabe in 40 Bänden in Verbindung mit Konrad Burdach und anderen herausgegeben von Edward von der Hellen - Cotta, Stuttgart und Berlin, 1902-1907 *Der junge Goethe*, neue Ausgabe in sechs Bänden besorgt von Max Morris, Insel, Leipzig, 1912. *Faust*, 2 Bde. - K. J. Schröer, Heilbronn, 1888.

GRIMMELSHAUSEN, HANS JAKOB CHRISTOFFEL VON - *Grimmelshausens Simplicissimus Teutsch* - herausgegeben von J. H. Scholte (Neudrucke Deutscher Literatur-Werke, 302-309) Niemeyer, Halle/Saale 1938.

HÖLDERLIN, FRIEDRICH ... *Gesammelte Werke*, 3 Bde. - mit Einleitung herausgegeben von Wilhelm Böhm - Diederichs, Jena, 1911.

HOFFMAN, ERNST THEODOR AMADEUS - *Dichtungen und Schriften*, Gesamtausgabe in fünfzehn Bänden herausgegeben von Walther Harich, Weimar, 1924.

KERNER, JUSTINUS - *Sämtliche poetische Werke* in vier Bänden, herausgegeben mit einer biographischen Einleitung und erläuternden Bemerkungen von Josef Gaismaier-Hesse, Leipzig, 1905.
Briefwechsel mit seinen Freunden, 2 Bde. herausgegeben von Theobald Kerner - Einleitung und Anmerkungen von Ernst Müller - Stuttgart und Leipzig, 1897.

KLINGER, FRIEDRICH MAXIMILIAN - *Stürmer und Dränger*, erster Teil, Klinger und Leisewitz (Deutsche National-Literatur, Bd. 79) herausgegeben von August Sauer - Stuttgart, n.d.
Dramatische Jugendwerke in drei Bänden, herausgegeben von Hans Berendt und Kurt Wolff, Leipzig, 1913.

LENAU, NIKOLAUS - *Sämtliche Werke und Briefe* in 6 Bänden, herausgegeben von Eduard Castle, Insel, Leipzig, 1910.

Lenz, Jakob Michael Reinhold – *Gesammelte Schriften*, 5 Bde. herausgegeben von Franz Blei, George Müller, München und Leipzig, 1909.
Lessing, Gotthold Ephraim – *Werke* – Vollständige Ausgabe in fünf und zwanzig Teilen, herausgegeben von Julius Petersen und Waldemar von Ölshausen in Verbindung mit anderen – Bong, Berlin und Leipzig, n.d.
Sämtliche Schriften (Achtzehnter Band-*Briefe, Zweiter Teil*) herausgegeben von Karl Lachmann, vermehrte Auflage besorgt durch Franz Muncker, Leipzig, 1907.
Novalis – *Schriften* 4 Bde. im Verein mit Richard Samuel herausgegeben von Paul Kluckhohn, Bibliographisches Institut, Leipzig, n.d.
Schelling, Friedrich Wilhelm Joseph – *Werke*, Auswahl in drei Bänden herausgegeben von Otto Weiss, Leipzig, 1907.
Schiller, Johann Christoph Friedrich von – *Sämtliche Werke*. Säkular Ausgabe in 16 Bänden. In Verbindung mit anderen herausgegeben von Eduard von der Hellen, Cotta, Stuttgart und Berlin, 1904.
Uhland, Ludwig – *Werke*, 2 Bde. herausgegeben von Ludwig Fränkel, Bibliographisches Institut, Leipzig und Wien, n.d.
Wackenroder, Wilhelm Heinrich – *Werke und Briefe* in zwei Bänden, herausgegeben von Friedrich von der Leyen, Eugen Diederichs, Jena, 1910.
Wieland, Christoph Martin – *Oberon* mit Einleitung und Anmerkungen herausgegeben von Reinhold Köhler, Brockhaus, Leipzig 1868.

II – *Critical and Reference Works (including Periodicals)*

Alt, Johannes – *Grimmelshausen und der Simplicissimus*, Beck, München, 1936.
Baumgartner, Ulrich – *Adelbert von Chamissos Peter Schlemihl* – Frauenfeld, Leipzig, 1944.
Böckmann, Paul – *Hölderlin und seine Götter*, Beck, München, 1935.
Borchert, Hans Heinrich – *Der Roman der Goethezeit* – Urach und Stuttgart, 1949.
Buchwald, Reinhard – *Führer durch Goethes Faust-dichtung*, Kröner, Stuttgart, 1949.
De Boor, Helmut – *Die höfische Literatur* (De Boor-Newald – *Geschichte der Deutschen Literatur*, Bd. 2), Beck, München, 1953.
Dilthey, Wilhelm – *Das Erlebnis und die Dichtung*, Leipzig, 1907.
Düntzer, Heinrich – *Uhlands Dramen und Dramenentwürfe*, Hoppe, Leipzig, n.d.
Errante, Vincenzo – *Lenau*, Mengen, 1948.
Garland, H. B. – *Storm and Stress*, London, 1952.
Heinzmann, Franz – *Justinus Kerner als Romantiker*, Tübingen, 1908.
Hewett-Thayer, Harvey, *Hoffmann: Author of the Tales*, Princeton, 1948.
Hiebel, Frederick – *Novalis*, Francke, Bern, 1951.
Keferstein, Georg – *Parzivals ethischer Weg* – Weimar, 1937.
Kerr, Alfred – *Godwi*, Berlin, 1898.
Korff, H. A. – *Geist der Goethezeit* – 4 Bde., Leipzig, 1923-1953.
Mann, Thomas – *Chamisso* (Essays of three Decades) – Knopf, New York, 1948.
Michel, Wilhelm – *Das Leben Friedrich Hölderlins* – Schünemann, Bremen, 1949.
Müller, Ernst – *Hölderlin, Studien zur Geschichte seines Geistes*, Kohlhammer, Stuttgart und Berlin, 1944.
Pascal, Roy – *The German Sturm und Drang*, Manchester University Press, 1953.

REED, EUGENE E. – *The Union of the Arts in Brentano's Godwi*, The Germanic Review, Columbia University, April 1954.
ROSANOW, M. N. – *Jakob M. R. Lenz* (Deutsch von C. von Gutschow), Leipzig, 1909.
RUNGE, EDITH AMELIE – *Primitivism and Related Ideas in Sturm und Drang Literature*, Baltimore, 1946.
SALZBERGER, L. S. – *Hölderlin*, Yale University Press, New Haven, 1952.
SCHAPLER, JULIUS – *Chamisso Studien*, Arnsberg, n.d.
SCHNEIDER, FERDINAND JOSEF – *Goethes Satyros und der Urfaust*, Niemeyer, Halle/Saale, 1949.
SILZ, WALTER – *Early German Romanticism*, Harvard University Press, Mass., 1929.
Problems of „Weltanschauung" in the Works of Annette von Droste-Hülshoff, PMLA, September 1949 (Menasha, Wisconsin).
STRICH, FRITZ – *Natur und Geist der deutschen Dichtung* (*Die Ernte, Franz Muncker zu seinem 70. Geburtstage*), Niemeyer, Halle/Saale, 1926.
TONNELAT, ERNEST – *l'Oeuvre Poêtique et la Pensêe Religieuse de Friedrich Hölderlin*, Didier, Paris, 1950.
ULMER, BERNHARD – *Eichendorff's „Eine Meerfahrt,"* Monatshefte, March-April, 1950, University of Wisconsin.
WEAVER, CHARLES P. – *The Hermit in English Literature from the Beginnings to 1660*, Nashville, Tenn., 1924.

INDEX

absolute, 90, 92.
Absolute, das, 94.
Adamas, 95.
Adamskinder, 60.
Adelheit, 106.
Ahnung und Gegenwart, xiii.
Alabanda, 95.
Alba, 73.
Albanians, 99.
Alexandria, 84.
Alfonso, 88, 102, 114, 117.
Al-Hafi, 36ff., 43.
Alhard, 72.
Almansor, 91.
Alonzo, 114.
Alma, 114.
Alpine, 118.
Altgermanische Religionsgeschichte (de Vries), xii.
Alvarez, 114.
Amanda, 91.
Ambrosius of Kamaldoli, 85.
America, 26.
Amor, 75.
Amor Dei (Kolbenheyer), 118.
Anachoreten, xii, 111.
anchorite, xiii, 111.
An den Mond, 59.
An die Verstummten, 118.
Anfortas, 2, 3, 4.
Anmutige Gegend, 51.
Anacreontic, 26, 30.
Annamarie, 19.
Annonciata, 67.
Antonio, 92f., 114f.
Arab, 46.
Ariosto, 85.
Arsinoe, 15.
Asia, 98.

Asian, 84.
Asiatic, 106.
Askalon, 46.
Aufklärung, 13.
Aventiure, 3.

Ballade vom Wandersmann, Die, 118.
Balduin, 73, 78f., 87, 89.
Bamberg, 84.
Barcelona, 111.
Baroque, 116.
Beatrice, 105.
Bechstein, Ludwig, 32.
Bergwerke zu Falun, 110.
Berka, 59.
Berlin, 10, 48.
Bernardo, 55.
Bild der Mutter, 68.
Bismark, 19, 21ff.
Blasius, 26ff., 52.
blue flower, 109.
Braut von Messina, die, 48, 57, 105.
Brentano, xiii, 66, 82, 118.
Bruderzwist, 49.
Bulemanns Haus, 118.
Buschy, 26.
Bürger, 31-36, 108.

Cäcilia, 75.
Carthusian, 20.
Chamisso, 47, 77, 88.
Charlemagne, 32.
child, 96.
childhood, 96, 99.
Christian, 24, 31ff., 43, 46.
Christian hermits, 84.
Christianity, 12, 47, 97.
Christentum, xii.
Cidli, 60.

classicism, 118.
Contessa, 84.
Count Robert, 77, 89.
crusades, 103.
curse, 75, 106.

Dante, xi, 85.
Dämon, 76.
Defterdar, 37.
Devin du Village (Rousseau), 56.
Dervishes, 37ff., 82.
Derwisch, Der, 36.
Deutsche Mythologie (Grimm), 32.
Deutsche Sagen, 32, 106.
deutscher Wald, 34.
Dietwald, 106.
Diotima, 95, 99.
de Vries, Jan, xii.
Doctor Marianus, 113.
Don Diego, 77, 88f., 92, 102, 114, 118.
Don Manuel, 105.
Donna Isabella, 27f.
Droste-Hülshoff, Annette von, 78ff.
Düntzer, Heinrich, 106.
Dürer, xii, 33, 35, 112.

Early German Romanticism (Silz), 94.
Earth-Spirit, 92.
East Prussia, 118.
Eckart, 106.
Eden, 74, 77.
Eginhard, 106.
Egypt, 52.
Eichendorff, xiii, 49, 77, 88, 93, 102, 110, 114, 118.
Eine Meerfahrt, 49, 70, 102, 114.
einfache Leben, Das, (Wiechert), 118.
Einsiedel, Der (George), 118.
Ekkehard (Scheffel), 118.
Eldorado, 114.
Elysium, 90, 94.
Emperor Ducius, 84.
Eudora, 16.
Engelbrecht, 19ff.
English Romanticism, 97.

Epos, 72.
Eremit, 17.
Eremit, Der, 10, 31.
Erinnerung, 104.
Erlebnis, 18, 19.
Ernte, Die (Franz Munker, Festschrift) xi.
Errante, Vincenzo, 77.
Erwin, 59, 63, 87.
Erwin und Elmire, 54, 66, 87.
Europe, 115.
Eusebio, 69.
Evagrius, 85.
Ewig-Weibliche, das, 111, 113.

Facetiae, 12.
Fanny, 49.
Fatime, 37.
Faust, 80, 111ff.
Faust II, 51.
Faustian, 48, 52.
Fausts Leben, Thaten und Höllenfahrt, 80.
Faustus, Doctor, 33.
Ferdinando, 64.
Filnek, Wolf von, 46.
Fortunatus, 48.
Frau Hohl, 60.
Fräulein Schatouilleuse, 59.
Fühlbarkeit, 30.

Gedanken über die Herrnhüter, 10.
Geist der Goethezeit (H. A. Korff), 95.
George, Stefan, 118.
genius of history, 102.
German literature, xii.
German literary tradition, 52.
German Romantic Lyrics (Silz, W.), 116.
German Romanticism, xi, 66, 106.
Germanic art, xii.
Germanic gods, xi.
Germanic landscape, xii.
Germans, 95.
Germany, 101, 103.
Glasperlenspiel, Das, 118.

125

Glücksäckel, 51.
gods, xii.
Godwi, 66, 82, 88, 109, 118.
Goethe, 13f., 17ff., 25, 28, 30f., 35, 54, 59, 60, 66, 68, 87, 111.
Goldener, 88, 109.
Gothic, 32.
Grail, 2f., 6.
Greece, xi, 95.
Greek, 95, 97.
Greek independence, 99.
Gregor, 118.
Gretchen, 113.
Grillparzer, 79.
Grimaldi, 64, 78f.
Grimm Brothers, 32, 106.
Grimmelshausen, 1, 4, 6, 116.
Guelfo, 64.
Guevara, 6.

Hackelberg, Hans von, 32.
Hanau, 4.
Hannoverian, 32.
Harfner, 68, 111.
Hauptmann, Gerhart, 118.
Heidemann, 21.
Heinrich, 24.
Heimatlosen, Die, 36, 71, 88, 108.
Helgoland, 109.
Herder, 13, 67.
Hermes, 16.
hermit-pose, 118.
Herz, 59, 64, 87.
Hesse, Hermann, 118.
Hewett - Thayer, Harvey, 84.
Hiebel, Frederick, 103.
Hingabe, xi, 2.
history, 103.
Hitzig, 84.
Höchst, 3, 4.
Hochwald, Der, 118.
Hodefield, Lady, 69.
Hoffmann, E. T. A., 71, 77, 80, 84, 110.
Hohenzollern, 14, 77, 88f., 92, 101f., 117.

Hölderlin, 71, 91, 95, 119.
homecoming, 99.
Honesta, 59.
Hörnerstadt, 11.
Hummel, 19.
Hüon, 91f.
Hyperion, 18, 21, 48, 53, 95ff., 118f.

Ideen zu einer Philosophie der Natur, 94.
Iliad, 60.
Innerlichkeit, xi.
Insanity, 84.
insulate, 88.
Isabella, 105.
island, 88.
isolate, 88.
Ither, 3.

Jericho, 46.
Jew, 39.
Joduno, 68.
John, 49, 51.
Joseph, 66, 109.
Josephus Famulus, 118.
Juliette, 64.
junge Goethe, Der (Morris, Max), 13, 54.

Kamilla, 64.
Karolina Berkley, 26, 29.
Kerapolis, 11, 12, 17.
Kerners Briefwechsel, 108.
Kerner, 21, 36, 88, 91, 108, 115, 118.
Ketzer von Soana, Der, 118.
Klärchen, 55.
Kläusner, 32f.
Klausnerin, 1.
Kleinen, Die, 4, 19, 21, 24, 30, 31.
Kleist, Ewald von, 30.
Klinger, 25ff., 30f., 36f., 64, 66, 80.
Klingsohr, 105.
Klopstock, 60, 113.
Kloster bei Sendomir, Das, 79.
Klosterbruder, 36, 41, 74, 77.

Knan, 5.
Kolbenheyer, Erwin Guido, 118.
König Eginhard, 89, 106.
Koreff, 84.
Korff, Hermann August, 66, 95.
Kunersdorf, 48.

Lady Katharine, 26.
La Feu, 26ff.
Lambert, 109.
lay hermits, 66.
Lehrgedicht, 12.
Leiden, 95.
leit-motif, 97.
Lenau, 31, 66, 77, 87.
Lenz, 4, 19-31, 59, 66, 87.
Lessing, xiii, 12ff., 17ff., 31, 35ff., 53, 74, 77, 80f., 118.
Lessing, Karl, 36.
Leviathan, 80.
Lili, 54.
Loki, 1.
Lorenzo, 79.
Louis, King of Sicily, 82.
low Saxon, 32.
Luchs, 109.
Luise, 29ff.
Lyric poets, 118.

madness, 70, 85f., cf. insanity.
Mann, Thomas, 218.
Märchen, 48, 82, 88, 109.
Märchendichtung, 108.
Märchen und Sagen (Bechstein, Ludwig), 32.
Maria Magdalena, 113.
Marie, 66, 103.
Maria, 77.
Marionetten, Die, 31, 66, 77.
Marlowe, 33.
Martarillo, 82.
Masslosigkeit, 18.
Mater gloriosa, 111, 113.
Mathilde, 105.
Meerfahrt, cf. *Eine Meerfahrt*

Messias, Der, 113.
Messina, 105.
Mina, 50.
miner, 103.
Minne, 1, 2.
Minnedienst, 2.
Mönche, xii.
Mönchtum, xii.
monk, 79.
mons serratus, 111.
Montserat, 111.
Morgenrot, 110.
Morris, Max, 13.
Moslem, 37, 41.
Mt. Etna, 105.

Nachtstück, 77.
Nackte Heilige, Der, (cf. wunderbares Märchen, etc.), 71ff., 82, 87.
Nathan der Weise, 10, 13, 36ff.
Naturanschauung, 14.
Naturfrömmigkeit, 95, 97, 98, 118.
Natur und Geist der deutschen Dichtung (Strich, F.), xi.
Naturreligion, 97.
Naturvergeistigung, 94, 111.
New Testament, 97.
Nietzsche, 118.
Nile Delta, 84.
Nördlingen, 5.
Novalis, 29, 71, 77, 88, 91, 93, 101, 103, 107, 117.
Novellen, 66, 84.
Novellist, 85.

Oberon, 35, 70, 78, 88f., 109, 114, 117.
obsession, 83.
Ode on Intimations of Immortality, 97.
Odenwald, 59
Ofterdingen, Heinrich von, 35, 70, 71, 78, 92, 101, 107, 109, 117.
Olimpia, 55.
Orient, 82, 103.
Orla, 118.
other-worldliness, 90.

Ottilie, 68, 69, 74.

pagan, 106.
Parzival, xi, 4, 6, 21.
Parzival, 92.
Pater ecstaticus, 112.
Pater profundus, 112.
Pater seraphicus, 113.
Patriarch, 13, 41.
Paul, 89, 106, 110.
Penthesilea, 114.
pessimism, 101.
Petrarch, 61, 85.
Pflanzenwelt, 99.
Philistines, 14.
Pisan Fresco, 111.
plant, 95.
Plettenberg, 60.
Poetry, 70.
Poggio, 12.
Problems of "Weltanschauung" in the Works of Annette von Droste-Hülshoff, (Silz), 72.
Prussia, 26.
Psyche, 15, 16.
Ptolemeus, 84.

Quarantana, 46.

Rahmenerzählung, 72, 96.
Ramsay, Susanna, 5.
Rascal, 50.
Rat Krespel, 86.
Recha, 45.
Reinhardstein, 69.
Religion, Die, 10.
religion, 96.
Rembrandt, 118.
Repans de Schoie, 2.
Rezia, 91.
Ritter Gluck, 86.
Ritter, Tod und Teufel, 33.
rococo, 54.
Robinsonaden, 89.
Robinson Crusoe, 89.

romantic, 64.
Romantic, 96.
Romanticism, 34, 53, 71, 88, 94, 95, 117, 118.
Rosa, 56.
Rothe, 59.
Rousseau, 16, 56, 62.
Rousseauistic, 61.

Sagengestalt, 111.
Saladin, 37.
Salamis, 101.
Salas y Gomez, 88.
Samaritan Woman, 113.
Satyros, 10, 13ff., 21, 25ff., 30f., 52, 66.
Schatten, 48.
Scheffel, 61, 118.
Schein, Scheinwert, 48.
Schelling, 94.
Schildeis, 106.
Schiller, 105.
Schlemihl, Peter, 20, 47ff., 84.
Schlemihlium, 52.
Schionatulander, 1.
schöne Seele, 60.
Schröder, R. A., 118.
Schröer, 112.
Schutzgeist, 91.
Schweizer Lexikon, xii, 52.
Senne, Werdo, 66, 74, 78f., 87, 90.
Serapion, 80, 84.
serapiontisches Prinzip, 71, 84, 86.
Serapionsbrüder, 84.
Serpentin, 109.
Seven-League Boots, 51.
Shakespeare, 63.
Sicilian hermit, 82.
Sigune, 1, 2.
Sililie, 88, 109.
Silz, Walter, 72, 94, 116.
Simplicissimus, 1, 4, 30, 81, 89, 116.
Simplicius, 5, 10, 11, 28, 46, 64.
Singspiel, 58.
Sittah, 39.
solide, le, 48.

Spain, 26, 27, 111, 117.
Spanish, 114.
Spanish knight, 88.
Spessart, 5.
spiritualization, 78, 82, 90, 92, 94.
Stella, 59, 60.
Sternbald, xiii.
Sternfelss von Fuchsheim, 5.
St. Anthony, 80.
St. Francis, 35.
St. Jerome, xii, 35, 112.
Strassburg, 13.
Stifter, 118.
Storm, 118.
Storm and Stress, 7, 14, 15, 18, 19, 31, 53, 118.
Strich, Fritz, xi, xii.
Sturm und Drang, 10, 25, 31, 52.
Sturm und Drang, 19, 20, 26, 30, 53, 55, 61, 117.
Sunday, 32.
Swabian Romanticism, 107.
sylphs, 92.
symbolism, 101.

Tabor, 47.
Templar, 41.
terza rima, 77.
Teufel, 41.
Theatilde, 72.
Thebaid, 53.
Theban Desert, 84.
Thebes, 52.
The Hermit in English Literature from the Beginnings to 1660, xii.
Thmuis, Bishop of, 84.
The wild Huntsman, cf. *Der wilde Jäger*, Hackelberg.
Thirty Years War, 65.
Thuringian Forest, 59.
Tieck, xiii.
Tirol, 84.
Todessehnsucht, 71, 83, 88, 91, 108, 111.
Trakl, Georg, 118.

Trevrizent, 2, 3, 6, 10, 11, 18, 20, 21, 47, 66, 89, 92, 114, 118.
Triuwe, xi, 1, 2.
timelessness, 107.
Titania, 89.
Tunis, 91.
Turks, 95.

Über die Romantik, (Uhland), xi.
Uhland, xi, xii, 89, 106ff.
Ulmer, Bernhart, 114, 115.
Unendlichkeit, 90.
Urpflanze, 1.

Valerio, 56.
Vaucluse, 61.
Vaterland, 103.
Verenus, 76.
Vergeistigung, 90, 92, 94, 112.
Vermächtnis des Arztes, Das, 72.
Vicar of Wakefield (Goldsmith), 56.
Virgil, xi.
Virgin and Child, 73.
Voltaire, 13.

Wackenroder, 71, 82, 84, 87f.
Wahn, 60.
Wahnsinn, 70, 79.
Waldbruder, Der, 59ff., 66, 87.
Waldeinsamkeit, 107.
Waldner, Henriette von, 59.
Waldvater, 36, 88, 108ff., 118.
Wanderer zum Morgenrot, Die, 109.
Walter, 72, 78ff., 87, 103.
Wanderer, xi.
Wanderers Nachtlied, 59.
Weaver, Charles P., cf. *The Hermit in English Literature*, etc.
Wellner, 66.
Weltseele, 92.
Walzel, Oskar, 48.
Werther, 19, 29, 30, 59, 60.
Westphalian, 32.
Widukind, 32.
Wiechert, Ernst, 118.

Wild- und, 60, 88ff., 102, 117.
Wild, 26ff.
Wild- und Rheingraf, 32.
wilde Jäger, Der, 31ff., 108.
Wilhelm Meister, 68.
Wodan, 32.
Wolfram, 1, 4, 6, 118.
Wordsworth, 97.

Wulff, Fredrik, 61.
Wüstenväter, 53.
wütendes Heer, 32.

Zarathrustra, 118.
Zukunft, 105.
Zwillinge, Die, 64-66.

www.ingramcontent.com/pod-product-compliance
Lightning Source LLC
Chambersburg PA
CBHW031316150426
43191CB00005B/253